I0017221

JULIAN DELPHIKI

UPDATED
EDITION

CONTENT MARKETING
&
ONLINE VIDEO MARKETING

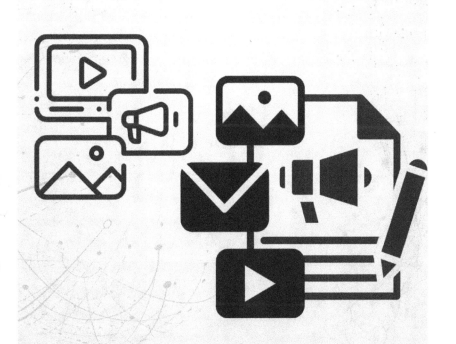

CONTENT MARKETING AND ONLINE VIDEO MARKETING

Master your content strategy and develop your online video marketing

- Julian Delphiki -

Copyright © 2025 Julian Delphiki

All rights reserved. No part of this publication may be reproduced, distributed, or transmitted in any form or by any means, including photocopying, recording, or other electronic or mechanical methods, without the prior written permission of the publisher, except in the case of brief quotations embodied in critical reviews and certain other noncommercial uses permitted by copyright law.

Content marketing and online video marketing / Julian Delphiki – 1st Edition

ISBN 9798647283269

INDEX

PART I

CONTENT MARKETING

STATE OF CONTENT MARKETING

CONTENT 'TIKTOKIZATION'

The rise of TikTok has heralded a profound transformation in how content is consumed and created. This phenomenon, often dubbed the "tiktokization" of content, is characterized by the proliferation of extremely short, often no longer than three-second, videos. The platform's explosive growth has forced creators and marketers alike to adapt, focusing on capturing attention instantly with flashy, dramatic, and highly engaging visuals. This shift underscores a broader trend in digital media: the move towards bite-sized, high-impact content that can be consumed rapidly and repeatedly.

In this new landscape, the traditional long-form content is increasingly giving way to snippets designed to be immediately gratifying. The brevity of TikTok videos aligns perfectly with the dwindling attention spans of modern audiences, who are inundated with information and entertainment options. To stand out, content must be visually striking and emotionally compelling right from the start. The first few seconds are crucial; they must captivate the viewer or risk being swiped away.

The impact of this shift is evident across all social media platforms. Instagram introduced Reels, YouTube launched Shorts, and even traditional media outlets are experimenting with ultra-short clips. This trend isn't merely about reducing the length of videos; it's about optimizing every second to deliver maximum engagement. Flashy transitions, bold text, and dramatic hooks are now standard elements, designed to keep viewers glued to their screens.

This emphasis on brevity and impact has significant implications for content creators and brands. The challenge lies in condensing a message into a few seconds without losing its essence. Creativity and innovation are paramount; each second must be meticulously crafted to ensure it leaves a lasting impression. The pressure to deliver compelling content quickly has given rise to new forms of storytelling, where a single glance or a quick motion can convey a complex idea or emotion.

Moreover, the tiktokization of content reflects broader cultural shifts. It mirrors our increasing preference for instant gratification and our reliance on visual media to communicate. In a world where time is a precious commodity, the ability to distill content into short, powerful bursts is not just advantageous but necessary. This trend also highlights the democratization of content creation; anyone with a smartphone can now produce and share videos that have the potential to go viral.

However, this shift towards ultra-short content also raises concerns. Critics argue that it can oversimplify complex issues and contribute to a culture of superficiality. The focus on quick, flashy content might overshadow deeper, more nuanced discussions. There is a risk that the constant pursuit of attention-grabbing moments can lead to sensationalism, where the line between information and entertainment becomes increasingly blurred.

Despite these concerns, the tiktokization of content is here to stay. It represents a fundamental change in how we communicate and consume media. As platforms continue to evolve and adapt to this new paradigm, the challenge for content creators will be to find the balance between brevity and depth, ensuring that even the shortest videos can deliver meaningful and impactful messages. The future of content creation will undoubtedly be shaped by these dynamics, as we navigate the ever-changing landscape of digital media.

The tiktokization of content has a profound impact on content creators and brands, reshaping their strategies and approaches in several significant ways. This shift towards ultra-short, high-impact content brings both opportunities and challenges, requiring a fundamental rethinking of how messages are crafted and delivered.

Content creators now face the challenge of capturing attention within just a few seconds. This demands a high level of creativity and innovation. Each video must be meticulously planned to ensure it stands out in a crowded digital space. The use of eye-catching visuals, engaging hooks, and dynamic editing techniques is crucial to make an immediate impact. The rapid consumption rate of short-form content means that creators must produce content more frequently to maintain visibility and engagement. This can lead to a more demanding production schedule, requiring efficient workflows and constant ideation to keep audiences interested.

Short videos are often designed to encourage quick interaction, such as likes, shares, and comments. This can result in higher engagement metrics compared to longer content, providing creators with more immediate feedback and opportunities for virality. However, it also means that content performance is closely tied to its ability to quickly resonate with viewers. The algorithmic nature of platforms like TikTok means that well-crafted content can quickly go viral, reaching millions of viewers in a short time. This offers creators the potential for rapid growth in audience and influence, often surpassing what might be achieved through traditional media.

Brands must adapt their marketing strategies to fit the short-form content model. This involves creating advertisements and promotional material that are concise, engaging, and tailored to capture attention quickly. Traditional advertising methods, which often rely on longer narratives, need to be reimagined for this new format. Audiences on platforms like TikTok value authenticity and relatability. Brands must adopt a more genuine and transparent approach, often collaborating with influencers who already have a strong connection with their audience. This can help in building trust and fostering brand loyalty. The fast-paced nature of short-form content means that trends can emerge and fade rapidly. Brands must be agile, constantly monitoring social media trends and being ready to adapt their content strategies accordingly. This requires a keen understanding of the cultural zeitgeist and the ability to react swiftly to new developments.

The lower barrier to entry for content creation means that brands are now competing not just with other companies but also with individual creators for audience attention. This heightened competition necessitates a sharper focus on quality and originality to stand out. Platforms that host short-form content provide detailed analytics, allowing brands to better understand viewer behavior and preferences. This data can be leveraged to refine content strategies, target specific demographics more effectively, and measure the success of marketing campaigns with greater precision. Creating short-form content can be more cost-effective than traditional advertising campaigns. The lower production costs, combined with the potential for high engagement and virality, offer brands a more efficient way to reach large audiences without a substantial investment.

One of the primary challenges for both creators and brands is balancing the need for brevity with the desire to convey meaningful messages. This often requires distilling complex ideas into simple, yet powerful, visual narratives. The emphasis on short, attention-grabbing content can sometimes lead to oversimplification of messages. This can be particularly problematic for brands and creators dealing with complex or nuanced topics, where important details might be lost in the quest for brevity.

The demand for frequent content updates can sometimes compromise quality. Both creators and brands must find ways to maintain high standards while keeping up with the rapid pace of content production.

The tiktokization of content is reshaping the digital landscape, offering new opportunities and posing unique challenges for content creators and brands alike. Success in this environment requires agility, creativity, and a deep understanding of audience dynamics, as well as the ability to leverage the strengths of short-form content while mitigating its potential downsides.

GEN AI, A TOOL TO RULE THEM ALL

Generative AI is a transformative tool that fundamentally alters the paradigm of content creation. This technology, capable of producing text, images, music, and even video, is revolutionizing how content is conceived, developed, and delivered. With its ability to generate vast amounts of material quickly and efficiently, generative AI shifts the balance from manual, labor-intensive processes to automated, streamlined workflows.

The implications of this shift are profound, touching every aspect of the creative industry.

At the core of this transformation is the unprecedented speed and scale at which content can now be produced. Traditional content creation often involves lengthy brainstorming sessions, drafts, revisions, and approvals. Generative AI, however, can produce high-quality content almost instantaneously. This rapid production capability allows creators to explore more ideas and variations in a fraction of the time, fostering greater experimentation and innovation. The efficiency gains are particularly significant in industries where timely content is crucial, such as news media, marketing, and social media.

Moreover, generative AI democratizes content creation. It lowers the barrier to entry for individuals and small businesses that may lack the resources for extensive creative teams. With AI tools, anyone with a basic understanding of the technology can generate professional-grade content. This democratization opens up the field to a more diverse range of voices and perspectives, enriching the cultural landscape with a wider array of narratives and styles. It empowers creators by providing them with tools that enhance their capabilities, allowing them to focus on higher-level creative and strategic tasks.

The impact of generative AI extends beyond just the quantity of content. It also enhances the quality and personalization of what is produced. AI algorithms can analyze vast amounts of data to tailor content to specific audiences, ensuring that it resonates more deeply with target groups. This level of customization was previously unattainable at scale, but AI makes it feasible to produce personalized content en masse. Brands can now engage their audiences with highly relevant and timely messages, improving customer satisfaction and loyalty.

However, the integration of generative AI into content creation is not without challenges. One significant concern is the potential for homogenization, where the unique human touch and creativity might be overshadowed by AI-generated content. While AI can mimic human style and tone, it often lacks the depth of emotion and authenticity that characterizes truly compelling content. Creators must find a balance, using

AI as a tool to augment rather than replace their creative vision. There is also the ethical consideration of AI-generated content, particularly in ensuring transparency and authenticity in what is produced and shared.

Generative AI also raises questions about intellectual property and originality. As AI systems learn from existing data, the line between inspiration and replication can become blurred. This necessitates new frameworks for copyright and intellectual property rights, ensuring that original creators are adequately credited and compensated for their work. It's a new frontier that requires careful navigation to protect the interests of human creators while embracing the efficiencies and possibilities that AI offers.

In conclusion, generative AI is a game-changer in the realm of content creation. It brings unparalleled speed, efficiency, and personalization to the process, opening up new possibilities for innovation and democratization. However, it also presents challenges that must be addressed to maintain the integrity and authenticity of creative work. As the technology continues to evolve, the key will be in leveraging its strengths while mitigating its potential downsides, ensuring that the human element remains at the heart of content creation. The future of content is undoubtedly intertwined with the advancements in AI, promising a landscape where creativity and technology coexist to produce richer, more diverse, and impactful narratives.

Generative AI is revolutionizing the landscape for brands and marketing agencies, fundamentally altering how they approach and execute their strategies. This technology's ability to produce vast amounts of personalized, high-quality content quickly is a game-changer. It allows brands to engage with their audiences in new and dynamic ways, shifting the paradigm from traditional, often static campaigns to dynamic, data-driven content strategies. The speed and efficiency of generative AI enable marketers to stay ahead of trends and respond to market changes in real-time, offering a significant competitive advantage.

For brands, generative AI enhances the ability to tailor messages to specific audience segments with unprecedented precision. Traditional marketing efforts often rely on broad messaging aimed at wide demographics, but AI allows for hyper-personalization. By analyzing consumer data, AI can generate content that speaks directly to individual preferences, behaviors, and needs. This level of customization fosters deeper connections with consumers, driving engagement and loyalty. Brands can deliver the right message at the right time, enhancing the overall customer experience and increasing the likelihood of conversion.

Moreover, generative AI streamlines the content creation process, reducing the time and resources required to produce marketing materials. This efficiency is crucial for marketing agencies that handle multiple clients and campaigns simultaneously. AI tools can generate various types of content—from blog posts and social media updates to video scripts and graphic designs—rapidly and consistently. This allows marketing teams to focus more on strategy and creative direction, rather than getting bogged down in the repetitive aspects of content production. The result is a more agile and responsive marketing operation, capable of adapting to clients' needs and market conditions swiftly.

Generative AI also brings a significant boost to creativity and innovation within marketing teams. By automating routine tasks, AI frees up human talent to focus on more creative endeavors. It can also serve as a source of inspiration, generating new ideas and approaches that marketers might not have considered. This symbiotic relationship between human creativity and AI-generated content can lead to more innovative campaigns that capture consumer attention and stand out in a crowded market. The ability to test and iterate on ideas quickly, using AI-generated variations, further enhances the creative process.

However, the integration of generative AI into marketing practices is not without its challenges. One of the primary concerns is maintaining authenticity and brand voice. While AI can mimic styles and tones, ensuring that the content aligns perfectly with a brand's identity requires careful oversight. Marketing agencies must balance the efficiency of AI with the need for genuine, human-crafted messages that resonate on a deeper level with audiences. This involves setting clear guidelines for AI-generated content and continuously monitoring its output for quality and consistency.

Ethical considerations also come into play. The use of AI in marketing raises questions about data privacy and consumer trust. Brands must navigate these issues carefully, ensuring that their use of AI respects consumer privacy and complies with regulations. Transparency about how AI is used in content creation can help build trust with consumers, who are becoming increasingly aware and cautious about their data. Marketing agencies must also consider the implications of AI on employment within the industry, as automation could impact jobs traditionally held by human content creators.

Generative AI is transforming the way brands and marketing agencies operate. It offers significant advantages in terms of efficiency, personalization, and creativity, enabling more dynamic and responsive marketing strategies. However, the successful integration of AI requires careful management to maintain authenticity, uphold ethical standards, and ensure the technology complements rather than replaces human creativity. As the technology continues to evolve, its role in marketing will likely become even more integral, reshaping the industry in ways that we are only beginning to understand. Brands and agencies that embrace this change, while addressing its challenges, will be well-positioned to thrive in the new digital marketing landscape.

PODCASTS EVERYWHERE

Not long ago, every business needed a blog to establish its online presence. Blogs were the cornerstone of digital marketing strategies, serving as platforms for companies to share insights, updates, and stories. However, the landscape of digital marketing has evolved rapidly. Today, having a blog is still essential, but it is no longer sufficient on its own. Businesses now also need an Instagram account and a podcast to stay relevant and competitive.

The rise of Instagram has revolutionized how brands connect with their audience. With its visually-driven platform, Instagram allows businesses to showcase their products, engage with customers, and build a strong brand identity. High-quality images, engaging stories, and interactive features like polls and Q&A sessions create a dynamic space for customer interaction. Instagram isn't just about selling; it's about creating a lifestyle that resonates with your audience. The visual appeal and instant feedback loop make it an indispensable tool for modern marketing.

Podcasts, on the other hand, have added a new dimension to how brands communicate. Over the past few years, the popularity of podcasts has surged, spanning various genres from true crime to influencer-driven shows. For businesses, podcasts offer a unique opportunity to literally give a voice to their brand. They provide a platform to delve deeper into topics, share expertise, and build a more intimate connection with the audience. Whether it's a brand discussing industry trends, interviewing experts, or sharing behind-the-scenes stories, podcasts can convey a sense of authenticity and authority.

The impact of podcasts is significant. They allow brands to reach audiences during commutes, workouts, and other daily activities, making them a versatile medium for content consumption. The conversational nature of podcasts helps in establishing a more personal and engaging relationship with listeners. For instance, a fitness brand could launch a podcast featuring workout tips, interviews with health experts, and motivational stories from users. This not only provides valuable content but also strengthens the community around the brand.

Brands can use podcasts to showcase their expertise and authority in their industry. By discussing relevant topics, sharing insights, and providing valuable information, brands can position themselves as thought leaders. For instance, a technology company could create a podcast series discussing the latest trends in artificial intelligence, featuring interviews with industry experts and case studies of successful implementations. This not only provides listeners with useful knowledge but also builds the brand's reputation as a knowledgeable and credible source.

Podcasts also offer a platform for storytelling, which is a crucial aspect of content marketing. Brands can share their origin stories, mission, and values in a way that resonates with their audience. Through compelling narratives and personal anecdotes, brands can humanize themselves, making them more relatable and trustworthy. For example, a sustainable fashion brand could create episodes about the journey of their products from raw materials to finished goods, highlighting their commitment to ethical practices and sustainability. This type of content can foster a deeper emotional connection with listeners.

Podcasts can be used to engage with the community and foster a sense of belonging among listeners. Brands can invite customers, fans, and influencers to participate in discussions, share their experiences, and provide feedback. This not only makes the audience feel valued but also creates a sense of community around the brand. A fitness brand, for instance, could feature success stories from its customers, interviews with fitness trainers, and tips from health experts. Such content can motivate listeners, create a supportive network, and reinforce the brand's image as a community-oriented entity.

Another significant advantage of podcasts is their versatility and convenience. They can be consumed while commuting, exercising, or doing household chores, fitting seamlessly into the busy lives of consumers. Brands can leverage this convenience by producing regular episodes that keep their audience engaged and coming back for more. Additionally, podcasts can be repurposed into other forms of content, such as blog posts, social media snippets, and video highlights, maximizing their reach and impact.

Podcasts are a multifaceted content marketing tool that can enhance a brand's visibility, authority, and customer engagement. By offering valuable insights, telling compelling stories, engaging with the community, and leveraging their convenience, brands can create a strong and lasting connection with their audience. In the evolving landscape of digital marketing, incorporating podcasts into the content strategy can provide a competitive edge and foster long-term brand loyalty.

While blogs remain a vital part of a business's digital strategy, the addition of Instagram accounts and podcasts has become crucial. Each platform offers unique benefits: blogs for in-depth content and SEO, Instagram for visual engagement and instant interaction, and podcasts for personal connection and expert storytelling. Together, they create a robust and multi-faceted digital presence that can effectively capture and retain the audience's attention. To stay ahead in the digital age, businesses must embrace these diverse channels and leverage them to tell their stories in compelling and innovative ways.

SOCIAL IS THE NEW SEARCH ENGINE

Search is shifting to social media platforms. Younger people, in particular, are moving away from traditional search engine results pages (SERPs) and turning to social media for more authentic, helpful answers to their questions. This trend is expected to continue in 2024, especially as social platforms integrate more search-focused features.

Consider this: 57% of Gen Z prefer TikTok over Google as a search engine. They find the answers on TikTok more relatable and personal, fitting their desire for authenticity. Google's own data backs this up, revealing that around 40% of young people begin their search on TikTok or Instagram. This significant shift is even reflected in the SERPs, with Reddit—known for its user-generated content and discussions—emerging as a major beneficiary of Google's August core update.

TikTok is spearheading this trend with innovative tools like the Keyword Insights feature, which helps marketers research social media keywords. The platform is also evolving into a comprehensive search hub, experimenting with integrating Wikipedia results and Google search links directly in its feed. Other social media platforms are not far behind. Instagram boasts a robust search function and shopping features, making it a key player in this new search landscape.

In 2024, creating social content optimized for discovery will be as crucial as optimizing for traditional search engines. However, the content must remain authentic and trustworthy, as the drive towards social media stems from users' desire for genuine, relatable information.

Understand the mechanics of social media search optimization. This involves learning how algorithms prioritize content and what users typically search for on these platforms. Compile a list of relevant keywords that your target audience is likely to use. Use tools like TikTok's Keyword Insights to identify popular and effective keywords in your niche. And finally, create search-optimized social media content. Capitalize in that content that is not yet covered   by other publishers.

RECYCLING / REPURPOSE

Great content is evergreen content. Unlike time-limited material that fades in relevance, evergreen content maintains its value and appeal indefinitely. This timeless quality ensures a better return on investment (ROI), as the content can be promoted continuously, reaching new audiences over time. The longer you can market a piece of content, the more exposure it garners, enhancing its value and impact.

Repurposing content involves taking existing material and rejuvenating it for various platforms and formats. This strategy maximizes the content's lifespan and extends its reach. For instance, imagine you wrote an in-depth blog post on a popular topic. It performed well, attracting significant page views and engagement. Why not extract some of the best parts and republish them? You could transform the most impactful quote into a Twitter post, create a catchy TikTok video summarizing the article, or redesign it as a downloadable PDF to share via your email list. This approach breathes new life into your content, making it accessible to different audiences in their preferred formats.

Consider a fantastic podcast episode you recorded with a special guest. By transcribing the conversation, editing it, and publishing it as a blog article, you can reach an audience that prefers reading over listening. This practice of repurposing isn't just about recycling content; it's about adapting and optimizing it for various consumption habits. People consume content in diverse ways: some prefer searching Google, others enjoy scrolling through social media, and some might come across your content through native ads on their favorite news sites. Repurposing ensures you meet your audience where they are, broadening your content's reach and effectiveness.

Moreover, AI generative tools have made content repurposing more accessible than ever. These tools can help you quickly adapt your existing content into different formats, eliminating the excuse not to repurpose high-performing material. Leveraging AI, you can efficiently convert a successful blog post into a series of social media updates, an engaging video script, or even an infographic. This technological assistance streamlines the repurposing process, allowing you to maximize the value of your original content with minimal additional effort.

In conclusion, repurposing evergreen content is a strategic and efficient way to maximize your content's impact. By continuously promoting and adapting your best pieces, you ensure they reach a wider audience and provide ongoing value. This approach not only enhances your ROI but also caters to the diverse consumption habits of your audience. In the dynamic digital landscape, repurposing content is a win-win tactic that ensures your valuable material remains relevant and effective over time. Embrace this strategy to extend the shelf life of your content and amplify its reach across multiple platforms.

THE BASICS OF CONTENT MARKETING

INTRODUCTION

I t should come as no surprise that the way in which businesses and their customers interact has evolved. With an almost constant connection online, there are more opportunities than ever for brands to communicate with their audiences.

Content marketing is the way in which businesses are responding to this changing landscape: it is a product of, and addresses the needs presented by, the 'digitization' of what, how, when and where customers get information relevant to their purchase decisions. Brands now have the opportunity to manage who they talk to, what they say, and when and where they do it, instead of being limited by the constraints of form and function imposed by traditional advertising.

In this lesson, we will take you through what content marketing is, how and why brands are using it, and the issues you should consider before diving in.

WHY USE CONTENT MARKETING?

The term "content marketing" can seem a little misleading. After all, there is no marketing without content, right? Even an ad or social media post consisting of nothing but a single word or your logo still contains content. To fully understand what we mean by content marketing, we need to look first at technology.

Thanks to the prevalence of mobile devices, each of us can access every bit of information we seek online, and we can do it whenever and just about wherever we want.

This has changed our relationship with the things we buy and use.

Today, the vast majority of shoppers begin their searches for products online, and the influences on their subsequent decisions are far more varied than they were in the past. Articles, reviews, user comments, various bits of how-to information, even entertainment content can factor into what we think and do.

As a result, customers do not care for traditional marketing any longer, so they are not looking to advertising to be a part of their research activities - in fact, a recent study found that over half of the respondents believed that websites should host fewer ads. The influence of people we like, respect, or know personally is often far more trustworthy and useful than messages from marketers. Just ask yourself, have you seen an ad recently that made you run out and buy something? And if you have, was this a rare exception?

Since customers are getting most of their information digitally, it should make sense to migrate advertising to those platforms, right? Only it does not. Most people actually dislike ads being inserted into their digital experiences, and that's where content marketing comes in.

Its premise is that the tools customers use to make purchase decisions can be made accessible to marketers if we stop thinking about selling something, and reorient ourselves to communicating the things that help customers reach some conclusion.

Traditional advertising was essentially a 'push' mechanism that offered businesses relatively few opportunities to form a dialogue with customers, so it made sense to pack every communication with the most memorable content possible. The ideas presented in ads had to survive the scrutiny and interpretation that occurred outside the view of marketers: all of the researching, vetting, and reviewing that happened between people.

However, these activities now happen online and in reach of marketers. Businesses can be a part of those activities, whether as an active participant in conversations, or as a source of information and expertise. The 'journey' that customers undertake – from the moment they first identify a need they wish to fulfill, all the way through to making a purchase – is now available to marketers, and digital insights allow for the identification and understanding of each step of it.

Content marketing represents the liberation of businesses from the constraints of the infrequent, limited communications activities of the past, and instead opens up a far wider range of communications options for companies.

In fact, the best way to think about content marketing is not just as a marketing tactic or tool, but as a powerful, entirely new way for you to think about, and act upon, your relationships with your customers. It is really a management system: it allows you to organize who you talk to, what you say, where and when you do it and, most importantly, define your expectations in measurable outcomes which will enable you to properly justify your communications expenditure.

In particular, content marketing enables brand marketers to see quantitative improvements from at least three core activities:

The first is in the ability to share substantive information. Freed from the necessity of guessing what might prompt a customer to buy something, brands can provide content that helps educate, inform, and illustrate product or service benefits. Combined with the greater number of digital platforms available to communicate through, and their relatively lower expense when compared to traditional pricing of print or digital ads, this opens up many more opportunities to communicate more information that would likely be of interest to customers.

The second quantitative improvement can be found in businesses' ability to be more agile. By 'agile,' we mean an iterative way of working that aims to enable companies to react quickly to any changes in environment and customer needs. A greater number of touch points, and a more open criteria for what constitutes 'content,' allows marketers to be more responsive to the changing needs of their customers, and react to newly

emerging challenges from competitors. These conversations are not just more substantive and frequent, but also more relevant.

And finally, content marketing allows you to reach new customers. In the past, there was often little budget put aside for trying to reach entirely new or uninvolved customers, as it would just take too long to convince them to buy, and the medium of advertising was not suited for this purpose. Now, marketers can use digital media to create content that might attract those customers; casting a wider net with information that might not sell anything, but instead start customers on the pathway to buying.

Beyond quantitative improvements, marketers who embrace these new opportunities to create and share content can also expect three qualitative benefits:

Firstly, content marketing can improve credibility. It has been said that sale pricing or discounts are what companies offer to make up for the lack of value customers see in their brands. However, content marketing can address this shortcoming head on by enabling businesses to maintain more meaningful and authentic conversations with their customers. Informed customers are usually better ones, because they are more likely to believe what you are telling them.

Next, content marketing can increase efficacy. Salespeople know that selling all the time is the worst possible way to sell – nobody purchases a product just because you want to sell it to them, but rather they do so because they want to buy it. Content marketing allows companies to 'collaborate' with customers in reaching their own purchase decisions.

The final qualitative benefit can be found in making brand value sustainable. Because content marketing can make your communications more efficient and reliably effective over time, it can make your customers' perceptions of value more sustainable over time. It is a departure from the 'episodic' nature of traditional marketing - giving customers discrete sales offers - instead, maintaining an ongoing conversation that supports their desires to make better purchase decisions. This is better for your brand, as an ongoing conversation with customers is more likely to be meaningful and reliable.

In short, content marketing is more than simply a marketing tactic, it is a management system which affords you control over your communications. And when it is done well, it can come with huge benefits to both brands and to audiences.

HOW ARE BRANDS USING CONTENT MARKETING?

There are a number of good reasons why content marketing is redefining communications for businesses around the world. But how exactly are brands using it?

Content marketing is a broad concept, and as a communications management system, it takes on a number of forms. Despite there being no "right way to do it," there are a few go-to ways that companies employ it to their advantage.

Let us look closely at three of those uses:

One of the keyways that content marketing is being used is to build customer awareness. One way that brands are doing this is by becoming a part of relevant conversations. For example, Amazon's Whole Foods publishes plenty of recipes and cooking tips on Pinterest. It is safe to say that few decisions on buying groceries are made independent of what you are going to make with those products. By inserting itself into that conversation, Whole Foods is making customers aware of the possibilities inherent in its offerings.

Or you might want to build awareness by contributing to inquiries. One way of going about this is by using quizzes, the way that Airbnb does. The brand challenges followers to identify pictures of locations it posts on Instagram, and rewards its audience with a link to its website with the relevant listings.

Alternatively, brands are building awareness through extending brand positioning across communications platforms using content marketing. By 'brand positioning,' we mean establishing or reinforcing the qualities that people regularly associate with a particular brand, in a way that helps define what the brand does and the benefits or purposes it serves.

The breakfast cereal-maker Kellogg's runs a good works program entitled "United Against Food Deserts," and supports work in urban gardens to provide fresh produce to underserved communities in the US. Links to its Twitter page not only provide updates on the program, but also link the audience to the company's other efforts - commercial or otherwise - including references to its position on key public policy issues, such as LGBT rights.

Much, if not most of this content would never appear in a 'traditional' ad, yet all of it is laser focused on building customer awareness.

A second way brands are using content marketing is to build customer loyalty. A keyway of achieving this is through addressing customer problems. Not only should this be done quickly, but also broadly - your solutions (and, ideally, your customers' satisfaction with them) should not only solve specific problems, but also become informative content for others.

A good example of this is Nike's Twitter service, @NikeSupport. Here, Nike not only provides immediate responses to posts detailing current user issues, but it also proactively posts solutions to issues before they have even arisen, such as notifying followers that the Operating System on their connected devices needs to be updated. Identifying opportunities to go beyond the immediate issue and provide extra value-adding content elevates every interaction into a marketing opportunity. Customer service is therefore a content marketing strategy that you can either embrace, or ignore at your peril.

Another tool for building customer loyalty is to recognize and involve customers. There are many examples of campaigns that feature user-generated content, or "UGC." For example, Land Rover created "Land Rover Stories," in which photographers document their adventures and share them with other customers. Every instance of user-generated content flips the old model of marketing on its head by allowing customers to tell their stories instead of having stories told to them, providing an authenticity which no marketing creative can compete with.

A third way to build loyalty is to use content marketing to stand for something. This is perhaps somewhat risky – taking a stand may offend as many people as it thrills. However, it is becoming increasingly necessary in a world that is not only connected, but in which customers expect more from their brands. In fact, a recent survey found that the majority of customers want brands to weigh in on social and political issues – topics that are relevant to a brand and its customers, but could be contentious.

For instance, outdoor gear-maker Patagonia's robust content marketing campaign centered on the preservation of the Bears Ears National Monument in the American West. This included a website, links for customers to post their concerns socially, and a sign-up for more information. This type of marketing might not sell any hiking shorts, but that is not the point; it deepens Patagonia's customer loyalty by standing for something in which its audience feel invested too.

Ultimately, the content marketing approach to customer loyalty is simple: talk to them as fellow human beings, not merely as buyers of your products or services.

Perhaps the most important way brands are using content marketing is in building their audiences. However, this is also the precursor to conducting your content marketing - the audience you possess and build through content marketing is itself an asset to your business. Content marketing is all about collecting audience data, and in turn, that data is what enables content marketing.

There is no public audience that is fully anonymous and uncounted in the digital world in which we all participate in some way or another. When we visit a website or social platform we do so with an identifier – a user or member name, an email address, a customer number – and many of our online activities involve entering that information and more in order to post, like, comment, share, or join.

As such, your business has the potential to know this public audience, however imperfectly, because you can capture that audience information and segment it in a variety of ways – be it by where you encountered them, how often they visit, what they do or say, or any number of other behavioral qualities.

This information can then be used to build models of what 'kinds' of customer they are in terms of their "journeys" towards purchasing your products or services. This is why content marketing is similar but not synonymous with public relations – both are focused on building relationships, but the "public" with which content marketing interacts is far more defined, known and tracked, than the public with which PR communicates.

The most straightforward example of audience building is encouraging someone to subscribe to your hosted content on Facebook, YouTube, LinkedIn, or on publishing sites like Medium. Of course, you need these audiences already so that you can share your content with them. This means that your content marketing strategy must also include a plan to capture, track, assess, and parse your audience data, so you can match the right content to the right people at the right time.

But remember, there is no definitive 'right way' to do content marketing, and the variety of ways in which brands are using it is vast. The important point to keep in mind is that content marketing is truly a management system, not just a new marketing strategy or tactic. It can change how you interact with any audience, whether that is your customers or other stakeholders.

WHAT ISSUES DOES
CONTENT MARKETING RAISE?

B y now, you should have a clear idea of what content marketing is, and the ways it is being used. However, before you dive into creating a content plan, it is important to consider some of the notable issues that content marketing can raise.

It is likely that you are already aware of the importance of online privacy, perhaps due to government action or any of the many well-reported hacks or breaches of data. Perhaps you have even been a victim of one yourself – it has been reported that 9 people have their personal data exposed every second of every day. Considering the importance of data within content marketing, privacy risks – both real and perceived – are crucial to factor into your content marketing development plan.

Specifically, if you are going to make a more concerted effort to track your audiences, and use that information to communicate more meaningfully with them, you need to make sure you have the appropriate security procedures in place in order to protect that data. This is not just a technical IT concern; it is also a process one. How many people in your marketing team have access to customer data? Do they access it remotely, and thus risk being hacked? What are the organizational limitations relating to their use of it?

It is also vital to keep abreast of new and emerging rules for how you acquire that data. For instance, government regulation such as the GDPR in the EU require you to do things like notify customers that you are tracking them and give them the opportunity to opt-out. Data security needs to be a priority within your content marketing project.

But remember, the concept of privacy is also subjective. Beyond government regulation, most individuals have their own opinions of what constitutes 'privacy,' and what does not – which means that you need to be sensitive to your customers' perceived notions of what you should know, and what you should do with that information. The rule here is: just because you can do something, does not mean that you should.

Beyond privacy, with the near infinite possibilities that content marketing presents, there is the constant threat of overuse or misuse.

Unsurprisingly, nobody really wakes up in the morning and wishes they received more communications, even from their favorite brands. On the other hand, due to the proliferation of platforms and the available real estate on them, there is a huge range of opportunities to distribute content.

It is important to find the delicate balance between these two issues. Whilst it is important to reach your audience, the last thing you want to do is push too much content at them.

The final issue to be aware of is metrics.

Measuring the effectiveness of your content marketing is directly tied to your understanding of your customers' purchase journeys, but it generally falls into four buckets:

The first is awareness. These metrics center around gaining an idea of the total size of your audience. This might include visits to your site or to the online publishing platforms on which you host your content, and broad metrics regarding your subscribers or followers.

Then, there's behaviors. What do they do when they visit? Do they like, comment, request, click through? These metrics should give a measure of your engagement levels.

Next, there's approval. These are metrics of endorsement - after registering their reactions, how many people forward or share your content? It is important to remember that measuring approval will be approximate – users may be forwarding content they hate, for example.

And finally, there's purchase, the metrics that ultimately legitimize your content marketing efforts. Which members of your audience end up purchasing from you and how?

Depending on the context, this may concern trial requests or donations, rather than 'purchases' specifically.

When it comes to measuring the effectiveness of your content marketing, choosing the right metrics is not just an important step along the way, but a potential issue, too. There is no single, established way to measure the benefits of content marketing, in the same way that there is no single way to evaluate the effectiveness of your marketing overall. As such, you need to be sure you are measuring things that evidence actions that your business chooses to value, otherwise it will always beg the question of what the effort was really worth.

Of course, these concerns should not put you off pursuing content marketing. That said, being aware of the issues affecting the marketplace - and how your company should handle them going forward - is key to the ongoing success of your content marketing efforts.

TOOLS, RESOURCES, AND CONSIDERATIONS

INTRODUCTION

As we have seen, the best way to think about content marketing is as a management system, with the aim of providing information to customers at key points along their journeys towards purchase. No single element of this system actually makes a direct sale, but all of the components add up to encouraging not only sales but also a deeper and more reliable customer loyalty. As such, it may seem tempting to dive straight into building your content marketing plan. However, first, you need to gain an understanding of the things you will need in order to make it happen.

OWNED, EARNED & PAID MEDIA

There are three types of media through which you can deliver your content: "owned," "earned," and "paid."

Owned media is just what it sounds like… content that you publish yourself, whether that is on your website or via posts to pages you host on social media platforms, and can range from short Tweets to lengthy essays or videos. A physical paper brochure is an analogue version of owned media, as are live presentations your executives might make at events. Whatever form it takes, ownership means that you have complete control over what you communicate, and how much and how often you do it, even if you do not control the terms and conditions of the platform, how it will be shared, or how it will be interpreted by your stakeholders.

Owned media represents a powerful way of releasing your content into the world. However, this also means that it is perhaps the most overused and, interestingly, least effective tool in your content marketing arsenal because it opens up the possibility of marketers falling into three different traps.

The first is insularity. Everyone needs a good editor, and most of us need one who is both unbiased and somewhat ruthless. The ability to publish anything you want can lead to producing content that is far more relevant to what you or your internal stakeholders want to tell the world, instead of addressing what your customers truly want to know.

Alongside the risk of insularity comes the probability that your content creators will tend to overproduce your content, focusing too closely on what it should look like - instead of what it needs to be - in order to appear authentic and relevant. Prioritizing the medium over the message itself is a constant threat that should be kept in mind.

The third trap marketers may fall into when using owned media to distribute content is creating content that is evergreen but irrelevant. Complete control tends to lead people to produce content that has an extended shelf life in order to maximize the duration it can remain usable, in an attempt to maximize value – theoretically, at least. However, by doing this, the content often falls short of making particularly relevant points in order to minimize the risk of becoming outdated, or coming across as contentious.

It is fairly simple (if not a bit more complicated in practice) to avoid these pitfalls by challenging yourself with three questions:

• Would an independent third party publish what we have created?

• Does our content deliver the value, and not just the production qualities expected by our customers?

- And do we make a point that matters to our customers, and not just to ourselves?

Beyond your owned media channels, there is earned media. This encompasses all of the liking, sharing, reposting, and repurposing of your content by your customers. It is the mechanism by which engagement with your content is generated, and its quality and amount can be assessed.

As such, earned media is the affirmation of the effectiveness of your owned – and paid– content marketing efforts. If your owned content is effective, it should in turn drive your earned media. Unsurprisingly, many companies consider this close connection when they are planning content to be distributed on their owned platforms. This prompts a few key types of approach to content creation, each purposefully focused on earning exposure.

One of these approaches is thought leadership. This has become somewhat of a buzzword in most businesses these days, and often seems to refer to developing content that promotes a company's products or services, or comments upon the markets in which it competes. This can lead into the trap of only really appealing to those within the organization, and as such does not really prompt customers to affirm or share much of it.

But real thought leadership in a content marketing strategy is intended to do just that: challenge, inspire and otherwise motivate your audience to not just consume the content, but encourage others to do so as well. To achieve this, you might conduct original research, and build upon it to offer observations and forecasts that are interesting to your audience; or simply identify something that your customers do not know - or would find surprising - and share it.

Another way companies are driving earned media is through inserting themselves into current events, either by taking a position, or adding insights and nuance to news stories.

So, when an Intel exec speaks at an event about government's role in regulating artificial intelligence, they are not just participating in a public dialogue... but creating content that customers who follow Intel will recognize, value and, hopefully, share.

Others are turning to providing behind-the-scenes insights in order to earn exposure. Many companies, including Starbucks, Sephora, Harley-Davidson, and non-profits like the animal rights groups ASPCA, have used Facebook's live video streaming function to provide followers an insight into factories and other internal activities, which has great sharing value, especially for others who are similarly interested in these brands. The use of specific sites or technologies is not as important as this idea of going outside of the normal constraints of marketing communication, and finding new resources to share. It is important to also note that this content generally does not look anywhere near as scripted or polished as other content. However, this is not necessarily a drawback, as people tend to share stuff that looks and feels real.

Perhaps the most useful type of media you can use in your content marketing activities is paid media.

Whilst not identical to the 'traditional' form of advertising that content marketing has allowed marketers to break away from, the simplest way to think of paid media is... as a type of advertising. In the context of content marketing - whether that is through paying influencers to share your content socially, or by purchasing placements of your content in spots that may overtly appear as ads - the use of paid distribution has real relevance to our new model of how to engage with customers.

Take influencers, for instance. Most online communities have a small number of voices who command the largest followings within those groups. Sometimes they are celebrities, while other times they are just really good at finding and sharing content that their communities find interesting or useful. Many brands literally buy their endorsement of content, and there is no better way to consider such activities as anything other than a form of advertising!

Another example is the creation of content that appears to be editorial, but is not. These were referred to as "advertorials" in the past, but today are referred to as native or sponsored content. Companies pay for a spot in magazines, for example, in order to distribute content that they hope is relevant to the interests of their customers. Both of these examples illustrate that there is nothing wrong with buying your way into conversations, as long as you present content that actually contributes to them.

Taken together, owned, earned, and paid media are the building blocks of a content marketing campaign. Each tool can influence the others, and it is the ways that they work together that has so many marketers excited about the possibilities.

RESOURCE REQUIREMENTS

Before you build and deliver your content marketing plan, you will need an idea of the resources you will have to draw on. In general, there are five broad buckets of resources that you are going to require.

The first is data. Your content marketing activities begin and end with a recognition of who is in your community. Who is on your email lists? Who are your followers on the various social platforms? There are many more details to this understanding, but for now, it is important to acknowledge that you need resources to identify and manage your data.

Alongside managing privacy and security, this includes taking responsibility for making sure that you have the appropriate approvals for using that data (for instance, whether or not your audiences have opted-in to being contacted).

The second resource you will require is marketing integration. Questions of scope will loom large early on in your thinking. Content marketing could constitute the entirety of your outreach efforts – in fact, some would argue that is the only way to get the most value from it – though it is far more likely that you will conduct campaigns focused on defined segments of targeted customers.

With this in mind, what will you forego in order to fund what you wish to accomplish with content marketing? Understanding how your efforts will interact, as well as the cost tradeoffs, is key to meeting everyone's expectations.

Next, there's internal processes. Unlike the structure of traditional marketing, your content efforts may draw on different sources of information. This might mean gaining approvals from executives or departments not otherwise involved in marketing, and doing so more quickly than your established processes allow.

As such, enabling a content marketing activity means you will need to look outside of the marketing department in order to identify any new dependencies and make sure those affected are on board.

You will also need to consider ongoing management. Managing a content marketing program has a number of moving parts, from facilitating the planning to overseeing its execution as well as the surprises and issues that will likely come up. As such, you might want to consider a staffing solution that provides enough flexibility in time and responsibility to ensure its ongoing management.

And finally, there's external support.

Content marketing can involve resources beyond the confines of your organization, specifically: third party vendors and partners.

Your track record in engaging with such third-party service providers is crucial in determining their level of involvement in your planning and execution. Suffice to say that if you do not normally work with external partners, employing them for the first time to help on your first content marketing plan might not be the smartest choice. Instead, rely on your proven capabilities, and evolve from there.

If you do decide that you will need external support, you might elect to hire an agency to conduct your content marketing efforts on your behalf.

Naturally, there are some potential drawbacks to this approach. Firstly, if you consistently turn to external resources, you may not develop the required expertise in-house, and instead find yourself always relying on third party help – which could become costly over time. On top of this, most third-party agencies are still marketing firms, so you may lose out on the deeper insights from within your company that could influence the content you want to share. And finally, letting someone else do the work may remove the sense of shared investment in the success (or failure!) of your content that would help you improve your efforts over time.

Of course, it is not all bad news. It can be easier to outsource the work involved in your content marketing efforts; a firm specializing in the work should have an established methodology on which you could rely, meaning the work may get done quicker; and hopefully it would have a higher likelihood of success. Alternatively, you could elect to do the work in-house, which addresses the shortcomings of the outsourcing approach, but turns the benefits of going to an agency into risks for you to bear instead. Building up your content marketing capability could take time and involve a number of starts and stops as you learn the ropes. However, the longer-term benefit is the opportunity to develop and monetize your expertise and capability.

If neither of those options appeal, you might instead opt for a hybrid approach, which would involve picking and choosing from the first two options. This might mean developing a plan that allocates some tasks to third parties (such as creative development) whilst keeping others within your organization (perhaps data security or resource management).

You should aim to facilitate real collaboration with any third parties and your internal stakeholders to ensure a transferal of knowledge and a sense of shared ownership; and create an environment in which both 'sides' of the team feel encouraged to challenge preconceptions and actively adapt to the changing needs of your customers.

UNDERSTANDING YOUR ORGANIZATION

Before you put your content plan together, it is important to come to terms with what type of communications your organization is willing to embrace. Since content marketing is best understood as a management system – that is, it allows you to manage how, when, where and with whom you communicate – there are decisions that need to made, or existing conditions recognized and respected, before you initiate your development activities.

As such, before developing your content plan, it is important to ask yourself three questions. These have less to do with the substance of your marketing, and more to do with how your company is run.

In order to establish your business's limitations when it comes to communications, start by asking yourself: how free are you to advocate for customer needs?

If the assumption internally is that marketing is simply supposed to deliver the ideas and exact messaging that those responsible for branding have devised, then your content marketing campaign will be dead on arrival. In fact, doing content marketing poorly is probably worse than not doing it at all, because instead of your content simply being ignored, it could in fact prompt negative reactions from your customers.

Customers do not 'want' branded content, they want content from brands that is relevant to them. Capitalizing on this opportunity will likely require your company to say and show things that it might not do normally. Before you get started, assess its willingness to be flexible, which will require finding out whether you have the level of support needed from within the company.

Another question to consider: how will adopting an agile approach to content challenge your organization's preconceptions about marketing?

Successful content marketing relies on freshness and relevance, which makes the premise of 'evergreen' content seem somewhat damning to any strategy. Unfortunately, many marketing decisions around content creation are made based on how long it will 'work' for, with an eye on maximizing return on investment.

A successful program will require making more content, more often, so your organization needs to be prepared to support that approach; otherwise, you will find yourself asking for reviews or seeking approvals from stakeholders who will not necessarily understand why the last approvals were not sufficient.

The final question to consider is: how will your company react when things go wrong?

Content marketing is not inherently a risky endeavor, but your efforts to address real customer interests with relevant, timely content may result in some missteps. The challenge of being fast and authentic can lead you to produce the best possible content, but can also raise the chances of your content being received in a way that you did not expect or intend.

If your company says it encourages risk and recognizes failure as a tool for learning how to succeed, does it really mean what it says? You may want to come to terms with that reality, as the likelihood is that you will make mistakes at some point... but the benefit should come from learning from those mistakes.

Recognizing the limitations of your organization is vital to your content marketing being effective. Think carefully about your answer to each of these questions, as failing to answer all of them effectively could sink your content marketing before you even start.

Customer models and publishing your content

INTRODUCTION

As is hopefully evident by now, content marketing is much more than a marketing tactic - it is a management system, and it can and should change the way you communicate publicly, and quite possibly, within your company too.

At its core, it is company communications configured for the requirements of today's technology, targeted at the real needs of customers, and aligned with the principles that drive modern day brands. However, as with any business endeavor, before embarking on your content marketing journey, you should develop a well-thought out plan.

In this lesson, we will take you through how best to develop a content marketing plan, starting with developing detailed customer models, all the way through to publishing your content. We will then touch upon the key considerations you should keep in mind every step of the way.

PERSONAS AND THE CUSTOMER JOURNEY

So, how can you develop an effective content marketing plan?

Well, one of the best places to start is creating customer personas, or models of who you sell to. Much of the information you will use to do this may already exist within your marketing function, such as gender, age, income, and geographic location. You may want to go further and correlate this information with data on which customers are your 'best' ones, or create personas for your current highest return customers or the types of buyers you believe could be profitable for your business.

The key here is to start with literal descriptions of the key attributes of your customers.

Then, go beyond those factual details – the more you use the better – and add to them the fictional details that would describe who they are... literally creating their "personas" as human beings. But remember to keep it focused – you can quickly lose yourself in needless detail that might be imaginatively interesting, but not relevant to your business.

Instead, hypothesize key attributes of their lives, such as:

- Are they busy?

- What is their comfort level using technology?

- Do they make slow or quick decisions?

- Who do they rely on for input on their decision-making?

- Do they even enjoy shopping? And,

- Why does this particular persona do business with you?

Some go as far as to name their personas, which can help as shorthand when you plug them into your plan later on. You can always change any of your assumptions during the process, as well as add factual attributes to refine them. Consider creating a single page on each persona which describes who they are, why they matter to your business, and just as importantly, why you matter to them.

Beyond creating your personas, you will also need to develop models for their customer journeys.

If 'personas' are models of how certain categories of customers think and feel, your customer journeys are maps of their behaviors: of what they do, and when they do it. Consider the process that any of us goes through to reach a conclusion: our "journeys" involve collecting, vetting, and then using information to make decisions. This is often characterized as "awareness," "consideration" and then "decision."

Your goal here is to produce models that would describe the journeys your personas take to reach their decisions, and which contribute to establishing and maintaining their loyalty. Consider areas such as:

- The sources they use. What information do they care about most, and what sources of information do they trust? Do they use your website? What social media platforms do they use, and what other outlets do they rely upon?

- The process they go through when considering your product. Is purchasing based on an impulse or is it reasoned? What are the chronological dependencies – do they
- need to know about, say, environmental values before considering a product, or does that curiosity come much later in their journeys? How long does this process take?

- And, what their purchasing decision will 'look like.' What are the key signs that they are likely to buy, as well as junctures at which it is obvious you have lost them?

Once you have answered questions like these, the resulting models can be mapped as flow charts, running from "new" on the left, to "purchase" on the right, with boxes in-between that note each major step and its potential outcomes.

A number of companies that have initiated studies into their customers' journeys have found the conclusions useful, not only to their overall marketing, but even to other functions such as sales and product development. You might be surprised at how complicated these journeys are, and by mapping them, you may chart new ground for your business.

With your personas and journeys in hand, you should use this information to define the goal of your content marketing efforts.

This might seem obvious... surely, it is to sell stuff?

Well, actually no, your content marketing goal should be to influence one or more of those key steps in a customer's journey. Not all steps carry the same level of importance and, while advanced content marketing programs provide engagement along entire journeys, for your first few efforts you might want to pick just one step, and see if you can positively influence it. Ask yourself:

- Do you want to attract would-be customers to your brand – in other words, are you trying to get on their radar for the first time?

- Is there an identifiable point when your benefits are compared to those of key competitors?

- What about reality checks – steps when your customers look to third parties to substantiate your claims of value?

- Is the step you want to influence when they've all but decided to buy, and need help discovering how to do it?

- Could your step extend after purchase and involve help on using the product itself?

At this stage of your planning process, your goals can be somewhat vague, like "increase awareness," or "make it easier to discover benefits." Really, these are directional statements for your strategy, but it is important to choose goals that you believe will be impactful to the journeys you have created.

ASSETS AND RESOURCES

Once you have modelled your customers and the journeys they may take, as well as deciding the goal upon which you want your content marketing to focus, you should be in the position to consider the various assets and resources you will need to put your content marketing plan into action.

Begin by assessing your audience assets. This will give you an idea of who your content might conceivably reach, and where.

Who are the past customers who have shared contact information with you? What about website visitors who have read you company blog, white papers, or other content; and who is downloaded that content? Which website visitors have opted-in to receive communications from your business? Who are the users of social media platforms who have commented on or shared your content; and who has followed or liked you brand but been otherwise silent? These assets might even include users of traditional media sites who have engaged in some way with content relevant to your business.

When assessing your audience assets, your goal is to identify a group of people who use a media platform to do generally the same thing, and see if there are any correlations with steps in your customer journey models.

With the caveat that you first apply whatever privacy restrictions to your lists of assets as necessary, analyze your audience's behaviors and, importantly, the content behind them. Then, either map these behaviors against the step in the customer journey you want to influence or, if it is obvious, consider influencing the step that you see evidenced in your assessment, as you may discover some activity of which you were not aware.

For instance, if you are a food company, do a lot of people share recipe tips from your site? Do any of your past customers show up in commenting on your latest products, or perhaps offer advice on customer service?

You should strive to present your conclusions in simple language. For example, "Our X number of followers on Facebook engage with content about dairy-free baking recipes, and our Persona X followers care about giving recipe advice to other users, so we want to target them." Or "We have Y downloads of our guide to reducing food waste, and our Persona Y considers the environment before anything else, so that's our target."

The logic is quite simple, really: if something looks like it is valuable because it could track a step in your customer journey map, it makes sense to do it again, or do it more regularly.

You will also need to conduct an audit of your existing content - an analysis of what you already produce that generates the behaviors you would like to amplify. This is not simply a study of the substance of it, but rather a deep dive on how it performs online. The goal here is to produce a model of the content or types of content that work best for your customers. It can get a little complicated, but it can be broken down.

First, audit your website content by charting how each of your page URLs perform regarding visits. Some of your most wonderful blog posts may generate low traffic, whilst others prompt lots of visits. You want to understand why that happens by looking at keywords associated with them – are they optimized for search? – as well as attributes like grammar complexity and overall length, and consider the role of images.

This process can get very technical, but it is something that your website manager or service provider should either know, or be able to discover with relative ease.

Similarly, you will want to audit the content that you post on social sites, and determine the qualities that make them viewable and shareable. Remember that there may be different types of content that are used in different ways at points along your customer journeys.

Before you can put your content marketing plan into action, you will also need to determine the people, processes, and the technical tools you will require.

To successfully manage a content marketing program, you will need to identify and staff the key roles of creator, editor, publisher, and administrator of the plan. Whilst there can be more than one person operating in most of these roles, it is generally good to have a single administrator overseeing the program. Having a defined process is vital in ensuring program delivery, never mind its success, and your planning activities should give you a clear idea of the scope and substance of what you hope to accomplish.

For instance, if you have identified video as a key tool for your plan, you will also need to identify the resources you will need to create it; and the same goes for short or long-form copy. These roles also need to be authorized to accomplish their work, with required approval steps identified. This is probably no different procedurally to the way that you establish any other project or work group, other than the fact that it involves new steps and dependencies for your organization.

It is likely you will want to use Content Management Systems or "CMS" to help you create and distribute your content, as well as track its performance. There are providers that sell software systems which support the creation, editing, approvals and distribution you want to accomplish, though they take some getting used to. You can also purchase online management tools to track the performance of your content.

Initially, you may just want to use whatever online activity tool your company already has in place, as well as whatever production process framework already exists. You can always upgrade to more robust management tools if and when your needs justify them.

PUTTING YOUR PLAN INTO ACTION

Once you have formulated an approximate plan for who you want to reach, what you hope they'll do, the rough format or qualities of the content you believe will resonate most with them, and the resources required to create this content; it is time to start thinking about how you will put your plan into action.

When putting your content marketing plan into action, one of the best places to start is identifying the platforms you want to use. These platforms are where you want to reach your customers. The most common platforms used for publishing content are company websites, on which businesses have complete control over text, audio, and video segments. However, this also involves the challenge of bringing your audiences to those websites.

As such, you might want to use external platforms in order to drive customers to your own site to consume this content. Alternatively, as is more frequent these days, you might want to host your content on those external sites, allowing your audience to consume the content on whatever platform they are already using. For instance, many customers will read or share a post on Twitter without even clicking on the link to see the original or cited content. Some of the most popular external destinations for content include: Twitter, Facebook, Instagram, YouTube or Vimeo, LinkedIn, and Medium.

Depending on the platforms you choose, you will also need to consider how best to track your results. There are online activity tools available that can do it for you, but you can also use your existing tools or, depending on the scope of your project, even do it manually. Tracking visits, downloads, shares, and time spent on your site is easy, as those tracking mechanisms are built into whatever tool your company uses to host your site. Tracking behaviors on external sites is also pretty straightforward; just bear in mind it will take someone's time and attention to do it.

Some suggest that the sole purpose of your content marketing efforts should be to capture contact information so you can go about communicating with people directly, which would remove any need for specific measures to track them. This is not a hard and fast rule, however, since a considerable number of your existing and would-be customers presumably have no interest in getting contacted directly, let alone regularly; they prefer the freedom to interact with your brand at the time and place of their choosing.

However, there may be steps in one or more of your customer journeys at which it might make sense to try and capture that information. These approaches are not mutually exclusive. You should feel free to experiment; but just remember that customers are not specifically interested in giving you their information, so focus on offering value.

After you have decided where you want your content to appear, it is time to brainstorm ideas for the content you want to create, as well as its formats. These aspects are obviously interrelated in that certain types of content work best in certain media. For instance, humor often works best in visual media, as do how-to instructions, and detailed information is often presented through infographics. On the other hand, sometimes a point- of-view or even a helpful suggestion is best communicated by text. Your analyses earlier in this process should have yielded some insights on what works best for you.

For the purpose of your brainstorming stage, it can be helpful to consider formats as prompts. You have many options here, from blogs and infographics to webinars and podcasts, so you should always refer back to your emerging plan and match what is creatively possible with the needs and requirements of the people you are hoping to reach and influence.

Start small – with a single piece of content, or small set of it – to allow you to work through the basics of process and management.

When creating your content, consider Search Engine Optimization, and the overall importance of making your content "visible" online. There are too many examples in the world of companies producing great content that sits inert and unseen on their websites. You need to make sure to 'bake into' your content the words that you know are the terms your customers use when they search for content. Similarly, a quick study of the hashtags that your customers use most often online is also important because you will want to use them too.

The final step in a content marketing plan is pushing the button, pulling the cord - or doing whatever you do to publish content!

For anyone who is sent out an email blast, or approved something at a printer's office, you know this has the potential to be a harrowing experience. For those of you who have not, you need to be prepared for unintended and unexpected outcomes. For instance, your content might prompt a negative reaction or be interpreted in a way that you did not anticipate... or a technical glitch or human error might cause issue with your content or prevent it from being published altogether. Once your content is published, this is your opportunity to test your tracking procedure, as well as your chance to analyze "what" occurred and whether or not it met your goals. You may even want to see if your results on your target platforms influence outcomes on other ones – does your content prompt sharing in places you did not consider?

Once you have accomplished your test, or tests, you can begin to expand your program, identifying more customer touch points you would like to influence, and creating the content to do so. Your ultimate goal is an end-to-end management system that supports and tracks every step in your customers' journeys, getting them ever-closer to a purchase decision. You may never actually get there, or even influence every step consistently, but the benefits of your efforts will increase with each additional step you take.

Your content marketing efforts should not end with publishing. Learn from what worked - and what did not - and put these learnings to use as you expand your program to create ever-more effective content.

DEVELOPMENT CONSIDERATIONS

As you build out your content marketing plan, there are a few key considerations to bear in mind.

The first is to stay focused on overall business outcomes, and push connections between your metrics and the business itself.

Unfortunately, many of the metrics for marketing efforts, especially online, are somewhat self-referencing. Data tends to track actions that are presumed to have innate value – this is why we hear so much about "engagement," as if it is a business accomplishment in and of itself. It is not.

You need to constantly challenge yourself to find correlations between metrics that other departments use to measure success, especially the steps considered most-closely aligned with sales.

Beyond retaining a focus on business outcomes, you should also consider the role content marketing can play in your communications with employees. There is a lot of thinking these days that points to employees as a greatly underutilized audience of potential brand advocates. Their ultimate "purchase" may not be a product, but rather their increased loyalty and productivity. As such, your organization might benefit greatly from experimenting with reimagining employee communications as part of a content marketing plan.

You should also be mindful of ensuring quality over quantity. A quick search online will tell you how to plan and organize your content marketing so you keep to a publishing schedule, but the quality of your content is far more important than the frequency of your posting. Perceptions of credibility and value are precious and somewhat tenuous, and unless your customer personas are low-involvement buyers with low expectations, you want to make sure that what you share with them has the highest likelihood of meeting or exceeding their expectations.

And of course, you should always consider the important role of data.

As you develop your content marketing plan, it is crucial to consistently manage your data. The picture you have of who you are interacting with, and where, is the lifeblood of your ongoing efforts, and it can quickly get muddied if you are not careful about managing the data you collect. The clarity of the insights you derive from your data is more important than spinning the next wave of content, so take the time to get it right. Be a meticulous record-keeper and, if you are relying on a third-party content management system, make sure somebody in your organization is not just trained to use it, but is an expert with it.

Of course, it is not enough to simply manage your data – you will need to make sure it is helpful, too. Consider how your efforts will feed the funnel. Ultimately, most digital marketing schemes rely on being closed systems isolated from other practices within a business in order to function properly - and to be measured reliably, too. The very nature of digital identification and publishing matches people with content, and there is no more reliable mechanism for that than capturing and maintaining your own lists of customers.

So, whilst it would make sense for you to always focus on ways of building your database of identified targets, you also need to stay open to the necessity for reaching out to entirely new people. Your targeted content on a particular platform will not just be visible to people you have already identified, but a much wider pool of entirely new, potential customers.

This is classic 'lead generation,' and using content marketing to develop new opportunities could have a profoundly valuable impact on your business. A viewer of something you published might not return for a year or more, but at that point they could be ready to begin a customer journey with you.

Beyond keeping these considerations in mind, also remember that, even if you have some missteps, you will get better at content marketing with experience. As long as you stay focused on the strategic purpose of content marketing, and stay true to the premise that your customers deserve objectively valuable information, you will gain traction with your efforts.

PART II

ONLINE VIDEO MARKETING

AN ONLINE VIDEO STRATEGY

INTRODUCTION

The use of video as a tool for marketing and advertising has soared. On average, we are consuming more than one and a half hours of online video per day, and are increasingly choosing to stream video over watching television. In fact, we spend more time on sites with video, share far more video than text or image-based content, and retain more information that is conveyed through video compared with reading alone.

In these lessons, we will be covering online video marketing - the creation and distribution of video content as part of an overall marketing strategy; and an important subset of this: online video advertising, or the creation of video for paid-for, online ad spots.

To kick things off, we will be exploring the key things that you need to consider when building an effective online video strategy, from choosing the right platforms to host your video, to selecting the most effective video goals and KPIs for your efforts.

WHY CREATE VIDEO CONTENT

Given the buzz around video, it can be tempting to just dive in. However, any digital marketing campaign should start with a detailed strategic plan, and video marketing is no exception. Whilst video can be easy to create, many marketers significantly overestimate the impact of their video campaigns, and a quarter of businesses do not believe their current video strategy is generating a positive return on investment.

Creating an effective strategy will allow you to continually enhance and optimize your tactics, and ensure that your results are justifying your efforts. You will need to define clear goals, strategies and KPIs; to find the optimal channels - like Email or Social Media - and platforms - whether it is Facebook, YouTube, or LinkedIn - on which to host and distribute your videos; and to know how best to measure success on an ongoing basis.

The best place to start in forming your strategy is understanding the role that video plays within the customer journey.

The "customer journey" describes the different stages that current or prospective customers typically go through when deciding to do business with you.

But where does video fit into this journey?

Well, many customers use video as a starting point to research products or services, but many also say video serves as a significant motivator in their final purchasing decision.

In fact, nearly all marketers now recognize the merit of using video across the entirety of the customer journey – from awareness, all the way through to retention. An effective use of video incentivizes customers to look for further information about products and services, increases purchase intent, and improves conversion rates.

The first stage in the customer journey is awareness: your potential customer has identified a need, but does not yet know about your business, or that your products could help. At this stage, your aim should be to position your brand so that your prospective customers find out about you.

You should not focus on being too promotional or sales-oriented. The customer is still at a very early stage of thinking about making a purchase, so it is more important to create a mutual relationship based on shared interests. This could mean creating informational video content that would be interesting to your ideal customer profile, and placing it on the platforms that your target audience are most likely to use. If you sell gardening supplies, for example, you might offer tips for growing roses rather than immediately offering discounts on seeds and tools.

Then, there's consideration. The customer knows about you and your products, but is open to other options – perhaps they are considering product features, prices, or customer reviews. Here, it is vital to differentiate yourself from your competitors by showing the customer that you understand their needs, and demonstrating how you can help fulfil them.

It is still not time for blatant sales pitches. Instead, focus on demonstrating how your product works. This could include tutorials, product comparisons, guides, or even answering typically frequently asked questions. Examples of the actual results of your products are particularly compelling – these could take the form of case studies for B2B brands, or personal achievement stories for customers.

At the purchase stage, the customer is ready to buy, and it is your job to make it as easy as possible for them to do so. If your product is at all complex, videos that explain each part of the process can be beneficial. To build trust and credibility, you may want to include videos featuring customer testimonials, or an "About Us" story.

Finally, there's retention. This stage is all about building loyalty. To ensure that your customers get optimal use of your product, you might want to use video as some "welcome" material immediately after purchase. This could include usage instructions, "how to" clips, more advanced guides, or even demonstrations of potential upgrades and enhancements.

But remember, the customer journey is not always linear. Prospects may join and leave at different stages, and move in different speeds or directions. It is important to keep this in mind, but to motivate customers to convert, it can be helpful to include a call to action or "next steps" within each video.

Another key stage in creating an online video strategy is reviewing each of your digital channels for their potential roles in supporting customers along this journey, promoting your brand, and engaging your target markets.

Video can play an important role in your owned, paid and earned media categories.

Although they may not be the best for expanding your reach, your owned platforms - or the channels over which you have complete control - are great for generating engagement and relationships with existing followers.

Take your brand's website. Including a gallery on your site that lists all of your available videos with custom titles, descriptions and thumbnails could be helpful both for your visitors, and for your SEO efforts.

Email remains an excellent owned marketing channel, especially if you have a sophisticated CRM system that can tailor messaging to specific recipients. It is not a good idea to send video as an attachment, but embedding links to your various hosting platforms can be very effective. If getting readers to view your video is the main goal of an email, include a clear "play" button at the top of the message, and avoid allowing the rest of the content to become distracting.

Then, there is paid and earned media...

Paid advertising is usually the fastest way to grow your audience and to increase awareness of your brand, products, and services. As with any paid initiative, when embarking on online video advertising, it is crucial to plan carefully and take into consideration your target audiences, which platforms they prefer, and how to talk to them through video. You should also evaluate your results and test and implement improvements on a regular basis.

It is also important to include a clear call to action in each video, and to design your landing pages so they match the message of the ad and make it easy for the visitor to complete your desired outcome. Test different versions on different audience segments, make any necessary adjustments, and don't be afraid to discontinue poorly performing videos.

When video advertising is done well, viewers are more likely to remember something about the content or the brand, and to interact with the ad in some manner. To justify the cost of a paid campaign, you will most likely want relevant viewers to share your video.

The additional reach that your video receives through shares is known as your earned media. Every marketer dreams of having their video take on a life of its own and "go viral." Unfortunately, this does not happen very often, and it is usually impossible to predict which content will create that level of excitement. Utilizing paid media to expand your reach can be very helpful in increasing shares of your content: the more your video is seen, the further it is likely to spread.

To get the ball rolling on video shares you might consider pitching PR opportunities to place your video content in online magazines and other publications. Editorial coverage in credible sites can be an excellent way to boost your credibility and reputation.

In order to maximize the sharing of your video content, you might want to post your videos on your brand's social media pages. However, it is important to remember that you do not actually fully control or own your social media channels, meaning their terms and conditions can change at any time in ways that impact how your brand appears on them. Despite this, social media can still be a great place to host video, and a is channel that should not be forgotten.

CREATING A VIDEO STRATEGY

The most important part of your strategic process is forming a clear definition of what you are aiming to do through the use of video, and how this fits within your wider business goals and marketing strategy. When thinking about goals for your video marketing, you should consider both the overall goals for your wider campaigns, and specific goals for each individual video you create.

At a high level, businesses have reported that well-planned video content has contributed to increased levels of: awareness and understanding of products and services; brand familiarity and engagement; sales or other conversions; and overall website traffic. The use of video has also proved to benefit SEO efforts, and to reduce volumes of customer queries and the cost of providing technical support.

For individual videos, you might want to consider more specific goals, such as:

- Product purchases. Videos can include clickable buttons that link directly to product purchase pages and discounts.

- App or software downloads: For software publishers or mobile app developers, video can be used to persuade users to download their products.

- Lead generation: B2B companies can embed links to enquiry or contact forms for leads such as quotation requests, software demonstrations, beta testers or free trials.

- Subscriptions: If your product involves premium or exclusive video content for customers or paid subscribers, you may offer some of your content for free in order to encourage sign-ups.

- Or even donations: Nonprofit video publishers can also include online donation buttons.

These are only a few examples of the goals you may want to use. Once you have selected the right goals for your video efforts, it is time to set your sights on your KPIs.

The KPIs that you define to evaluate your video marketing efforts should be closely aligned with your chosen goals. It can be all too tempting to focus on tracking the number of views, or the number of completed videos, but unless they are related to your specific goals, these "vanity" metrics probably will not actually show you anything meaningful.

Instead, you should concentrate on only a few KPIs at a time that will best help you achieve your desired outcomes. When defining your KPIs, ask "Will our business be improved by tracking this?" If the answer is "No," it is time to look for a different metric.

There are a whole host of KPIs you may want to focus on, including (but by no means limited to):

•   Increasing traffic. This could include the number of click-throughs to your website from videos hosted on social media or circulated via email.

•   Increasing brand awareness. You might measure this by the number of new social media followers gained after watching a video, or the increase in branded searches.

•   Increasing brand engagement. This can be measured by the number of shares and comments, or by the amount of each video watched. You could also try surveys or focus groups to measure ad recall or brand familiarity.

•   Increasing sales and other conversions. It is very important to understand where all of the conversion opportunities are in relation to your video content; and to evaluate your success using the various conversion rates, how many people clicked through from a video link, or the amount of revenue you can attribute to video-generated leads.

Each KPI you use should also have an associated target so that you can be realistic in evaluating your results. This should also help you to gain management buy-in when making the business case for a video campaign.

For example, if you are hoping to attribute increased traffic numbers or improved conversion rates to your use of video, you could use achievable targets for these areas to develop projections of the impact of your video campaign on overall revenue. And if you have an idea of the cost of the campaign, and of your profit margins and lifetime customer value, you can then estimate the potential return on investment of your suggested strategy.

ONLINE VIDEO PLATFORMS

Once you know what you want out of your videos - your goals - and how specifically that should be expressed - your KPIs; you should use this to inform exactly where your videos will be hosted.

Using your owned platforms can be beneficial, but in order to increase the reach of your content beyond your existing audience, you will probably want to utilize online video platforms.

Online video platforms are services that enable users to upload, convert, store and playback video. There are several different types of platforms, all with different features and audiences; so, it is important to apply some strategic thinking when selecting a place to host your video. Do not try and be on every platform just because you can.

By now, it is likely that you will have come across marketing videos on YouTube and Facebook. Every day, we are watching over 100 million hours of video on Facebook, and over one billion hours on YouTube. The most viewed video on YouTube to date has reached over 5 billion views!

These are massive platforms. YouTube is globally considered to be the second largest social media channel, only behind Facebook, and is the second largest search engine after Google. Of course, it is owned by Google, which means that it is a major advertising channel through Google's skippable ads, and that success on YouTube is closely related to better positioning in the search engine's results page.

Beyond their magnitude, another thing both YouTube and Facebook share is how video is watched: the majority of the content uploaded to both platforms is actually watched on mobile devices.

But how exactly do they differ?

The key differences between YouTube and Facebook stem from why and how viewers use them.

On Facebook, visitors are primarily interested in social interaction, not in watching video - users are more likely to come across your videos by chance, and click on the ones that catch their attention. Because of this, shorter content often works better, as most video that users consume is on a momentary impulse. This also means Facebook users tend to have their sound turned off, so your video should work with or without sound. Captions can be particularly helpful, and have actually shown to increase interaction and conversion rates.

On YouTube, however, visitors are specifically seeking video content – particularly for education or entertainment - so the platform is better suited to longer-form or even serialized content, such as vlogs. Captions are less important here - because YouTube visitors are specifically looking to consume video content, they will most likely have their sound turned on.

In general, a video uploaded to each platform will perform differently over time. Videos uploaded to YouTube may take time to accumulate views, but after you reduce active promotion, attention around the video and in your channel is likely to continue. This means videos on YouTube tend to have a longer shelf life, and ultimately higher levels of engagement and return on investment. But it is not without downsides. Because there is so much content (and because YouTube's recommendation engine offers plenty of alternatives), it is all too easy for viewers to be lured away from your channel, or for them never to discover you at all. And if your video does become popular, it could attract inappropriate comments which may need to be moderated, or even disabled.

On the other hand, assuming you have the budget to promote it, Facebook will deliver more immediate views and social interaction. However, this will fall off quickly as your spending declines – viewers are typically quickly distracted by other items in their News Feed, and are less likely to engage further with your brand unless you continue to pay for ongoing ad positioning. But beyond being a tool for reaching a large, well-targeted audience and potentially creating a viral buzz, Facebook can be a great place to try out innovative formats – it is a leader in live and immersive video, and even has an algorithm that gives preference to virtual reality or 'VR' compatible content.

How you choose to allocate your resources between Facebook and YouTube will depend on your goals, your audience, and your budget. If you are looking for fast results for single pieces of content, Facebook might suit you better. If you are looking to build a more consistent following for ongoing content over time, YouTube is probably more useful. However, if a combined strategy is appropriate for your needs and you can afford it, a well-balanced campaign should seek to maximize the benefits of both.

Beyond YouTube and Facebook, there's Instagram. With its focus on lifestyle and in-the- moment experiences, Instagram serves as another popular platform that is well suited to some types of videos, including live streaming. Like Facebook, Instagram videos play with the sound turned off, so captions are recommended. It is also a primarily visual platform, so it is helpful to use bright colors and eye-catching creative in order to attract attention. You should also give some careful thought as to the keywords and hashtags you will attach to each video, as these will allow new visitors to find your content.

Instagram limits the length of any content to 60 seconds, so this is not the place for in- depth material. However, this is not necessarily a drawback - Instagram users tend to be restless and not interested in watching anything too long. On top of its 'grid' format, the platform also offers "Stories," allowing users to post content which is deleted after 24 hours. You might want to use this format for short, looped updates, behind the scenes looks at your company, or even exclusive offers or discounts that are only good for the lifetime of the video.

Next, there's Twitter. Videos on Twitter's timeline will auto play and attract attention, so very short but creative pieces may be viewed in their entirety as users scroll.

Posts on Twitter that include video tend to generate more retweets and favorites, and it is particularly effective for inviting user-generated content, or UGC, that highlights your brand. Because of its very ephemeral nature (tweets are very unlikely to be seen after about an hour), Twitter is also good for limited-time, immediate announcements or promotions using video. It is also a great place for short trailers and teasers of longer form content posted on other channels.

In contrast to other major platforms, LinkedIn is not really thought of as an obvious place for video marketing. However, its use as a video platform is predicted to increase, and it has major potential for B2B brands. Business-oriented content such as video profiles and customer testimonials can be added to company pages, and you can post video updates or share other video content related to your industry.

Beyond video marketing, LinkedIn also offers targeted video advertising, which can be useful for generating visibility with specific types of professionals or industries. Imagine you are looking to recruit new talent: to up the number of the right applicants, you may want to create a particularly effective recruitment video, and target it to the types of professionals you are seeking.

Available only as a mobile app and in vertical video format, Snapchat is great for momentary engagement, but tends not to be used for high-quality content because of its ephemeral nature. For brands, the most popular format on Snapchat is "Stories," which consist of 10 second video clips which are displayed for 24 hours, and a "Discover" feed of algorithmically sorted content from publishers and verified celebrities.

Advertising on Snapchat has been declining, especially in comparison with other platforms. Reasons for this include: price – Snapchat has positioned itself towards larger brands; and the demographic, which is largely composed of millennials. However, the 12-17-year-old age bracket prefer Snapchat to other social media platforms, easily outstripping their usage of Facebook or Instagram, so if teens are your audience (and they certainly consume a lot of video), you should certainly consider it.

There are a lot of platforms to consider when it comes to hosting video. Remember, do not try and be on every platform just because you can. Consider each platform's features, audience behavior and intent, and find the ones that are best suited for your business and your goals.

———— ○ · ● · ○ ————

FOCUS ON THE CONTENT

INTRODUCTION

Having outlined the online video marketplace, and covered the fundamentals of establishing an online video marketing strategy, now it is time to focus on creating video.

With so many creative options available, it can be hard to know what makes for effective video content, and especially what will work best for both your business and your audience. In this lesson, we will take you through the video creation process, covering the key decisions you will have to make.

TYPES OF VIDEO CONTENT

Many different types of content are well-suited to video marketing. Depending on the nature of your business and what you are looking to achieve, video content that could prove helpful in growing your business might include corporate stories.

Video is a great medium for telling your story and providing a "feel" for your brand, your leadership, and your employees. As well as staying updated on your latest news, customers like to understand your history and your background, the types of people who work for you, and their values and interests.

Here, you are trying to make the connection between your company, and the content that will strike an emotional chord with your target audiences - this should not be an exercise in "corporate speak."

Video is an excellent medium to convey informational content from your executives. Interviews are a great way to put a human face on your business whilst highlighting your brand's expertise and thought leadership within your field.

A vlog, which is a blog that is primarily created in video format, can be very good for this type of material. Depending on whether it is live streamed or pre-recorded, you may want to host this on your website, or on video-sharing sites such as YouTube or Vimeo. Vlogging is a powerful and engaging way of interacting with your audience, but as with any blog, you will need a strategic plan for your content and promotion, and to ensure you are consistent in your frequency of postings.

Explanations and demonstrations can be a great tool to help prospective customers, who often want to see the product in action before making their purchasing decision. Video is the ideal format for this: it is much easier to show how your product works visually than it is to explain in words.

"How-to" videos can also help to onboard new customers by showing them how to set up and use equipment for the first time. In fact, "how to..." is one of the most used search strings on YouTube. If your product is particularly confusing or complicated, producing troubleshooting or maintenance videos may even reduce customer service and support costs.

Beyond creating your own explanatory or demo videos, user-generated content can also be particularly successful. For example, tongue cleaner brand Orabrush created Orapup – a version for dogs. Dog owners were encouraged to post reviews on YouTube which included demonstrations of their animals using the scraper; with some reaching hundreds of thousands of views, constituting invaluable free marketing for Orabrush.

In fact, customer testimonials, or positive reviews by satisfied customers, can be very persuasive. Visitors tend to ignore or distrust written testimonials, but video versions featuring people that your prospects would consider peers, or who have similar problems to them that you have helped resolve, can convey much higher credibility.

Alternatively, you may simply want to focus on video that entertains. Whilst it is well- known that viewers will respond better to product placements in longer-form videos, many brands are experimenting with various different approaches to creating content with commercial appeal. In particular, the lines between video designed specifically for advertising or promotional purposes, and video as entertainment are becoming increasingly blurred.

A great example of this is fashion brand Kate Spade New York's popular #Missadventure campaign. Hosted on YouTube (with teaser spots found across social media), the series consists of short stories around the lives of fictional women, each played by well-known actresses. Whilst each video contains clickable links to buy the products featured, the content itself is not as obviously promotional. With its focus on entertainment over advertising, the series' audience grew to over 170 million views for the third series!

Whichever direction you decide to take your video content, you need to plan and document branding guidelines so that you can ensure consistency across all materials, regardless of who produces them. This should cover:

Your tone of voice. What type of personality and tone will your brand have? Is it always the same, or more formal or relaxed in some circumstances? If so, which ones? What about using humor?

If, when and how you will include your logo. Are there brand standards for the use of your logo which apply to video. For example, should your logo appear in every video? If so, should this be at the beginning, at the end, or as a watermark? A comprehensive guide should also detail the use of color and spacing around your logo.

Your brand colors and typography. In addition to standards for your logo, do you have guidelines for the use of colors, such as which should be used for the main text or headings, which can be used for shadows, and so on? What about rules around the usage and size of different fonts that apply to videos?

Whilst video-specific guidelines can go a long way, it is vital that your video portfolio fits into and supports your overall content strategy.

When you embark on creating video materials, you should take inventory of the assets that you already have, establish where the gaps are in the types of content and messaging that you need, and assess what it will take to fill in those gaps. Decide which types of content and calls to action would be appropriate for video; and be clear about the circumstances in which you will and will not use video, and why.

You should also include your video calendar within your overall content plan. This includes showing how the rollout and promotion of your video campaigns fits in with the schedules for other forms of content, as well as who will be responsible for each video project, its goals, target markets, and where it will be hosted.

INTERACTIVE VIDEO FORMATS

When it comes to video, it is not just a case of deciding the type of content you want to create. You must also consider the video formats that your content will appear in.

You will be familiar with standard pre-recorded, two-dimensional video. But beyond this, two formats that are becoming increasingly popular are live streaming and immersive video.

Live streaming refers to the simultaneous recording and broadcasting of events in real-time via the internet, and is growing rapidly. Be it on Facebook

Live, Instagram Live, Twitter's Periscope, or Twitch, viewers are intrigued by the unscripted, "anything-could- happen" interactions between participants; and the opportunity to connect with other viewers and offer immediate feedback or comments only provides further interest.

Live streaming can be used for a variety of corporate material, be it meetings and conferences, entertainment, interviews and Q&A sessions, training, and product demonstrations, or "behind the scenes" looks; and it is fast becoming a key tool for marketers looking to increase engagement and interaction. Users are increasingly choosing to watch live video over live TV, and many viewers would rather stream a brand's live video than read their social media or blog posts. In fact, Facebook Live videos are watched three times longer than regular ones, are commented on ten times as much, and are more likely to appear in timelines.

Live video can be easy to create, but as with any video content, you should take a number of steps to ensure its effectiveness.

First, keep it consistent. Whilst you want to attract viewers, you should make sure you are attracting the right viewers. Choose content that is interesting, but which also reflects your brand and your message. You should also broadcast at regular intervals so that your audience knows when you will be live.

Be interactive. Live streaming offers you the opportunity to interact with viewers in real- time: encourage them to comment, fill in a survey, vote in a poll, enter a competition, or even chat live with your presenters.

Finally, consider quality. You do not always need professional production – endurance race Tough Mudder's popular live streams are broadcast via mobile phones. A less polished, 'realistic' appearance can help to build rapport with your audience. However, you will need to make sure you have good sound and video quality, as well as a stable internet connection, to make sure you are not losing viewers.

Your live video can even drum up buzz after the broadcast has ended. To generate ongoing attention and maximize the return on your live streaming investment, consider posting both the full recording and edited highlights, and using paid advertising and social media to give it even more chance of being seen.

Alternatively, you might want to use immersive video.

As its name suggests, immersive video is designed to make the viewer feel completely 'immersed' in the content. Also known as "360-degree", these recordings are shot using an omnidirectional camera, or collection of cameras, to record in every direction at the same time. Users can interactively manipulate the angle of sight as they choose, which can be a somewhat choppy experience on desktop, but works particularly well when using virtual reality technology, or with a smartphone or tablet on which the video responds to the device being moved or swiped.

As for advertising, it proves a powerful medium: Hong Kong Airlines created a 360-degree video ad which aimed to give viewers a branded experience of business class. The immersive video was reported to be significantly more effective than the two- dimensional version, with viewers spending 9 times as long exploring the content, and a click-through rate of over 4.5%. And this is not limited to B2C brands. For example, B2B companies in areas such as engineering and manufacturing might provide prospective customers in the all-important shortlisting stage with a virtual tour of their factories or premises.

However, immersive video is expensive to produce, and some companies struggle to prove its effectiveness. If you do choose to produce immersive video, you should:

- Choose appropriate content. Make sure there is something appropriate and engaging in every direction, and that the content is appropriate for panning around. For example, a static interview probably is not the best choice.

- Avoid giving too much away. With 360-degree video, nothing is off limits... so avoid showing areas or practices that you want to keep confidential.

- Use high-quality editing. To provide the best viewer experience, storyboard carefully so that you know how your narrative progresses, where the interactions are, and how the various segments are connected; and ensure that content from different cameras is stitched together seamlessly. You may also want to include titles and captions to draw viewers to different areas.

The array of creative options available is vast. Remember that to be successful, everything from the type of content that you create and how it is used, to the format of the video in which it appears should be tailored in accordance with your ideal customer. Consider your target markets' video consumption preferences, including their interests, the platforms, and devices they are most likely to watch video on, and the length of video they are most likely to watch; and use this information to fuel your decision-making.

CREATING VIDEO

So, you have decided on the types of videos that you want, and have considered the types of content you think might work best. Now it is time to plan and create the specific content for each video.

As with any form of marketing message, the most powerful films tell a story that makes an emotional connection with the audience – whether that emotion is positive, such as happiness, passion, or gaining some feeling of power; or negative, such as sadness, alarm, or experiencing some type of loss.

Take British Airway's "Fueled by Love" video. The six-and-a-half-minute video told the heart-warming story of a cabin crew member's first visit to India, focusing on the flight attendant's special bond with an elderly passenger. The strong emotional narrative resonated with viewers, and the video garnered over 4 million views on YouTube as a result.

There are various narrative models for creating this connection. Charity appeals, for example, often start with an emotional hook. That hook is then supported by facts, and the video moves to a call to action. Another popular model is the "hero's journey." Here, the scene is set, something changes such that the characters have to take some form of risk or try something new, and the video resolves into a happy ending.

Whichever narrative model you use, storyboarding is a helpful technique for planning your video in detail. A storyboard consists of a number of squares containing sketches or illustrations for each slot; accompanied by notes, brief descriptions, or references to the dialogue of the scene. This allows every member of the team to see the video laid out; highlights any discrepancies in the flow; shows the locations, actors, music, and props needed at each stage; and generally, makes the filming process more manageable.

It is also a good idea to write a script, or at least an outline. Written dialogue provides direction to all of the crew, and offers a level of confidence to your actors – especially if they are employees that are not usually in front of the camera!

Another issue you will need to address is whether you want to create your videos yourself, outsource, or use a mixture of the two. Some of your video may require less effort in terms of production and editing. However, for videos that require a more professional look, you cannot afford to cut corners, even if it means paying for outside resources.

When it comes to outsourcing video creation, it is important to be clear about the options available to you.

Videographers are professionals with good equipment who have the expertise to film with appropriate sound, lighting, and so on. However, the creativity will still be down to you – you will need to provide a very clear brief, and you will probably still need to do your own editing.

If you are looking for more support than this, you might want to use a video production company. In addition to professional filming and editing, they can also offer a range of services, from strategic consultation to the activation and promotion of your video. Production companies can range in size, and standards of knowledge and ability vary, so do not be afraid to ask about specific expertise and access to a portfolio or references before deciding who to work with.

Finally, there's full-service agencies. These companies offer the full range of services for creating and producing video, from creative consulting through to editing and promotion; and often come with a broad spectrum of both equipment and expertise. Agencies can be a great choice: it can certainly be helpful to have input on your ideas from a knowledgeable third party, and they can even support your holistic marketing strategy by distributing your video across various channels. The most effective video ads are often made by experienced agencies like this; however, all this will come at a price (and you may even end up competing with other clients for time and attention).

No matter who you outsource to, it is important to stay actively involved in the process. Make sure that your chosen partner understands your goals, values, and desired messaging, and that the materials being created appropriately reflect these.

Alternatively, if you want complete control over what is produced, to own your own equipment, or to work within your own timeframes, you might want to form an in-house team who are responsible for creating your video content. But remember, this can still be an expensive option, especially if you need to find the right equipment and a team with appropriate skill levels.

If you do choose to bring your video creation in-house, you should not underestimate the importance of video editing. Editing your content is just as important as shooting it.

When editing video, there are a number of things you can do to make your content as effective as possible. Of course, this list is not exhaustive, but some helpful tips include:

Keep things moving. Audiences tend to get bored quickly if not enough is happening on screen, so either the action or dialogue needs to be compelling.

Focus on the first five seconds. This is the amount of time that you typically have to persuade a viewer to watch more – especially in the case of skippable ads.

And remember: less is more. If you are not sure whether some content is too much, cut it! Viewers tend to appreciate you getting to the point quickly, so make your message as streamlined as possible.

You will also need to think about the music you will use to set the mood, the calls to action that you will use to compel viewers, and how long your video will be. Given the average visitor's very short attention span, shorter content usually works better, so consider breaking up longer pieces into sections. And, as with any content creation, testing your videos on actual audiences will tell you a lot about what your target markets will like, and what they'll interact with.

How you decide to create your video will depend on the time and resources available to you. Ask yourself how much content you want to produce; what your current capabilities and available budget are; and what deadlines you are currently working with – finding the right partner, negotiating contracts, and communicating briefs can take some time.

Of course, your job does not end after you have created your video. Once you are ready to release it into the digital space, you will want to take steps to ensure that your video is distributed as effectively as possible.

YouTube is now the world's second largest search engine in its own right, and video results are prominent in Google and other organic search results pages. If you want your video to be found, it is important to bear in mind how it relates to search engine optimization.

Think carefully about your titles, descriptions, and meta tags. Do some research about what keywords your target audiences search for, and what words they use to describe your products and services. These should be used in your title, hashtags and in the video description, so that viewers can see exactly what your video is about – it is not helpful to use internal jargon that your audience does not use, or to call your video something vague like "How It Works."

The permitted length for titles varies between platforms but a general best practice is to keep titles to less than 70 characters to avoid being cut short in search results pages. Generally, whilst viewers' searches are often phrased as questions, they prefer titles that do not contain question words – the title "Mending a flat tire" is likely to generate more views than "How to mend a flat tire." Including a transcript of your video elsewhere on the page can also be very helpful for search engine optimization, as well as for visitors who prefer to skim read for a quick idea of what is included. You also need to consider your thumbnails. The thumbnail is the most important visual hook that attracts visitors – videos with thumbnails are clicked on far more in search results than those with text-only descriptions. Some platforms will automatically assign thumbnails, but if you have the opportunity to customize your own, try to incorporate people's faces, an image that conveys the story of the video, and bright or primary colors.

Finally, remember your sitemap. A sitemap is a file that contains a list of all of your site's pages and resources, and allows you to include information about videos. When made available to Google, this tells the search engine where all of the videos on your website are located and what they are about, so your video content can then be indexed.

—————— ○ · ◉ · ○ ——————

VIDEO ADVERTISING

INTRODUCTION

W hen it comes to video advertising, marketers' greatest concerns center around their relationships with ad networks, both in the fraudulent reporting of video views and in the positioning of ads next to offensive content. In this lesson, we will dive into these concerns, giving an extensive overview of online video advertising. We will then turn to how to measure the success of your efforts.

VIDEO AD FORMATS

A great deal of online video is used for advertising purposes, and publisher and social media sites accept video advertising in several different standard formats.

The most common is known as "in-stream." These play before, during or after the main video content:

Pre-roll ads are in-stream ads that play before the main video content. Because viewers generally want to see the content that follows the ad, pre-roll ads tend to be very successful in terms of completed views; making them particularly helpful for increasing brand awareness, and for launching new products or campaigns.

Many pre-roll ads are now skippable, known as TrueView ads on YouTube. As the name implies, the viewer can choose to skip the ad, either immediately or after a certain amount of time. Terms of service vary on different platforms, but as an advertiser, it is possible that you will pay only after the viewer watches beyond a minimum point.

On platforms where this is the case, you have essentially free advertising for a few seconds, and it is crucial to make the most of this time. The majority of viewers will skip the ad, and most will not remember the brand involved, so you should include your logo or a key message that will make an impression even if the ad is skipped.

Not only should you aim to make an instant impression, but your content should be engaging enough to encourage viewers to continue watching. To do this, you might want to use humor, like American insurance company Geico did. The highly successful campaign gave the impression that each ad was over after 5 seconds, at which point the ads became skippable. But, for viewers who decided not to skip, the videos continued, becoming funnier as they did so.

Pre-roll ads should be short. 15 and 6 second ads are becoming increasingly popular as they have the lowest impact on the viewer's time – a popular pre-roll format is YouTube's "bumper" ads: a fixed, six second ad slot. As a recommended rule of thumb, an ad should be no longer than 25% of the length of the content that it precedes.

Alternatively, there are mid and post-roll ads, which typically run between 15 and 30 seconds in length. Mid-roll ads play during content that viewers are already engaged in, and tend to have the highest completion rates. However, they are also rated as the most annoying. Post-roll ads play at the end of content, and have the lowest completion rates of all in-stream formats because viewers have little incentive to watch them.

Beyond in-stream ads, other popular video ad formats include in-read and display.

Also known as "outstream," in-read ads appear within blocks of text such as articles or editorial content, and are very popular on major publisher sites. Typically, they will auto play on mute as the user scrolls down the page, pausing when they are out of view. Due to their positioning 'within' content, they are very likely to be seen by viewers. However, because they do not play sound unless clicked, they are easily overlooked.

Display, or "discoverable," ads are pay-per-click ads that are shown at the top of a list of recommended videos, displayed to the right of the currently playing video on platforms such as YouTube and Facebook. On YouTube, these can also be shown in the search results.

Due to their placement alongside other video recommendations, they are designed to feel more like native content than ads. In general, you will probably need a fairly large budget for this type of advertising to make any significant impact. However, whilst they have the ability to be effective, these ads are the least likely to be seen by viewers of all the formats discussed, because they are not part of the primary focus of the page.

Of the standard video ad formats, we have discussed, there are pros and cons to each, and marketers report widely varying results. To get the most out of video advertising, you should test and evaluate your own results carefully to identify the optimal formats for your content.

VIDEO AD MARKETPLACES

Once you have your ad, it is time to distribute it. In order to place your video ads, you might work with a search engine marketing vendor, such as Google, which includes video in their format options. If you are a larger business, you might contract directly with publisher sites.

However, the other major option available is to place ads through the real-time buying and selling of video ads, known as programmatic. Now accounting for nearly 75% of all video ad spend, this automated method can be very convenient, and can give you wider exposure. However, programmatic buying can also leave you susceptible to issues such as brand safety and ad fraud.

Brand safety and other issues regarding offensive content has become a major talking point in the world of video advertising, especially with the prevalence of "fake news" on many social media platforms. Ads which viewers find offensive can negatively impact their response both to the surrounding content, and to other ads in the same space. Advertisers and publishers alike are becoming increasingly concerned about the nature of the materials that are being displayed - especially in the programmatic sphere where advertisers and publishers are not interacting with each other directly.

In fact, many major brands have withdrawn - or threatened to withdraw - content from YouTube after their ads were found displayed on channels promoting extreme or damaging views. And YouTube is not alone in this - Facebook has faced similar issues with brands for much the same reasons.

Of course, it can be difficult to establish exactly what constitutes "offensive" content; and it is not easy for platforms to monitor and categorize everything. So, it is important to take proactive steps to protect your brand's image: if you're using media buyers, ask them to detail the steps they're taking to avoid your ads being seen alongside negative content. If you are running campaigns in-house, carefully scrutinize the publishers you work with, and consider partnering with technology companies and solutions that can help protect your brand's online presence.

Beyond brand safety, there is the issue of ad fraud. Typically, this is understood to mean the manipulation of ad serving systems.

Criminals pose as sellers of legitimate ad impressions viewable by real people but instead employ various mechanisms that generate 'fake traffic' like page views, clicks or other seemingly human behaviors. This means the buyer ends up paying good money for impressions that never make it to their intended audiences, while the fraudsters walk away with the profits.

And because of the amounts spent on video in particular, fraudulent advertising activity on video accounts for nearly two-thirds of all ad fraud, with programmatic video being especially vulnerable. Desktop tools have been designed to detect and combat this, however criminals are increasingly targeting mobile ads, where these tools often do not work.

But it is not all bad news. The rates of ad fraud have been dropping, probably due to the level of pressure that advertisers are putting on the industry, resulting in better filtering processes.

Despite the dropping rates of ad fraud, the attraction for fraudsters to find new ways of beating the system is still strong; and you should keep the following considerations in mind when attempting to minimize its impact on your video ads:

Beware of certain ad formats. A technique used by fraudsters is to buy lower-value inventory on one network, repackage it, and sell it elsewhere at a much higher cost per thousand impressions, also known as CPM or Cost-Per-Mille, or CPT, Cost-Per-Thousand. Certain ad formats are particularly vulnerable: video banner ads are often sold as actual video inventory; and frequently, these ads are shown to bots rather than to real people.

Verify placements. The Tech Lab initiative, started by the Internet Advertising Bureau or the "IAB," encourages publishers to place a text file on their website which lists all of the companies who are authorized to sell their inventory, allowing advertisers to check for valid placements and sellers. The advertising industry also founded the Trustworthy Accountability Group or "TAG" which certifies vendors who take proactive steps to counter ad fraud. When deciding who to do business with, look for the companies that have been awarded the TAG seal of approval. You may also want to maintain your own allowed list of vendors you deem reputable, and block list those who you do not.

Monitor carefully. As criminal methods evolve, it is important to stay informed about developments in ad fraud techniques. A good, independent third-party software tool (that is, one independent from the ad networks) can monitor the placement and performance of your ad inventory.

Ad viewability is another key issue affecting the online video advertising landscape.

The concept of ad viewability refers to whether an ad could have been seen by the user it was served to. For example, if your ad is placed at the bottom of the page and the user does not scroll far enough down to see it, it is not viewable. This is important because you do not want to pay for an advertising impression if there was no chance that your video was seen, and for this reason, video ads are often charged on a CPVM, or "cost per viewable impression" basis.

Standards created by the Media Rating Council, or "MRC," and the IAB dictate that for a video ad to be considered viewable, at least 50% of the player must be in direct view of the visitor for at least two seconds – although the MRC is even considering raising this to 100%. However, not all publishers support these requirements, and there is no universally accepted standard on viewability.

Viewability rates have been rising recently, but it is still an important consideration in maximizing the effectiveness (and reducing the cost) of your video advertising.

To increase the viewability of your video ads:

- Set your own standards. If your budget is large enough, you can insist on your own minimum viewability metrics when paying for impressions.

- Work with reputable publishers. Even if your budget is not large enough to set your own rules, you can choose to do business only with publishers who abide by IAB or MRC standards. You may also want to ensure your publishers are measuring every impression, rather than just sampling.

And use optimal placements. Video ad players at the top or middle of pages are more highly viewable than those placed further down.

Finally, there is the issue of ad blocking. An ad blocker (which can be built into a web or mobile browser, or manually added by the user) is a piece of software that prevents ads from being displayed in a webpage. They are growing in popularity - Adblock Plus has been downloaded over 500 million times - and have caused the loss of billions of dollars in revenue.

The Coalition for Better Ads has researched the most annoying ad experiences on both desktop and mobile devices that are most likely to motivate customers to use ad blockers, and has used this data to create a set of standards for acceptable ads. Major publishing sites have joined the Coalition, and are no longer displaying ads which fail to meet these standards.

Video content which is likely to be blocked by publishers under these rules include in- read ads that auto play with sound, or ads with sound that are difficult to pause. Some have taken this further, and will also block ads placed in between paragraphs of an article, whether they are auto play or not.

Other best practices that help you meet these standards include:

Making pre-roll ads skippable. Pre-roll ads that are not skippable are seen as far more intrusive.

Targeting and personalizing content. Viewers can be especially annoyed by ads that are completely irrelevant to them, so it is important to target your audience, to personalize the content as closely as possible, and to ensure your ads fit with the content surrounding them.

Emphasizing production quality. Poor production quality can cause slow page load times and buffering, as well as taking up large amounts of data and bandwidth. Over a third of ad blocker users have cited this as their principal motivation for installing the software.

And avoiding the use of pop-up ads. Pop-up ads appear suddenly over the window currently in view, and can be incredibly disruptive. Need we say more!

The video ad space is complex, fast-growing, and evolving; with constant changes in ad formats, platforms, applicable devices, and ways of buying and selling ads. To create truly effective video advertising, it is vital to keep up with these changes, and adapt when necessary.

MEASURING SUCCESS

It can be difficult to effectively measure the impact of your investment in video. A huge amount of analytics data is now available, but how do you make sense of all the numbers, and derive useful, actionable intelligence?

A best practice is to benchmark your starting points for the KPIs you will be tracking before you start a video campaign. This will allow you to compare figures such as revenue, conversion rates, branded searches, and social media engagement before, during and after your videos run. If things are not working well, you will want to know where the problems are most likely to be – whether it is the content, the video quality and production, the targeting and promotion, or the calls to action and subsequent landing pages.

Let us take a look at some of the most common KPIs to measure, what they can tell you, and what actions you might take as a result.

In terms of KPIs for video, first and foremost there's reach. Although the raw numbers of people who see your video are not necessarily good indicators of business outcomes, they do give an idea of your success in improving brand awareness and visibility.

Hosting platforms often have varying definitions of a "view." If you are using their analytics data to monitor your view count, it is important to understand exactly what you are looking at in each case. Avoid making direct comparisons unless you are comfortable that these are valid. If you are using an agency to promote your video, ensure they are reputable and will not resort to buying you "fake views" which can skew your engagement and conversion metrics, and get you into trouble with your hosting platform. If the number of views does not meet your expectations, consider employing more proactive promotional tactics.

If your goal is around reach and brand awareness, it is also useful to track the number of times that your video is shared. This tells you how much your content appeals to your target audience, such that they are prepared to tell others about it.

If this metric is not achieving what you had hoped for, ask yourself whether your content is suitable for sharing. Does it require other context around it to make sense? Is it entertaining or educational? If you believe the problem does not lie with the content itself, consider being more proactive in asking your followers and influencers to share your video.

You might want to measure engagement. The primary measure of this is the duration of your video that is watched. If the majority of viewers click away after just a few seconds, then clearly the content has failed to capture them at all. If many viewers watch some of the video and then leave, perhaps it is too long, or too slow in getting to your call to action.

Do not worry if your videos are not always watched all the way to the end – average completion rates are in the region of between 65 and 75%, with over 75% being considered exceptional. It is important to think about the context of visitor actions before making a judgement on whether you have a problem. If viewers leave early, they may have actually clicked on an embedded link, or gone to find out more about your business.

However, if you are losing viewers immediately or very quickly, try making the introduction shorter, or experiment with removing logos and titles. If viewers are leaving well into the body of the content, consider cutting the content down or splitting it into smaller pieces. You could even experiment with using different voices, locations, or music.

Next, there's placement. Is your video well-located on the page? Is it relevant to the surrounding content? To answer these questions, consider looking at the "play rate" – that is, the number of people who proactively click on the video to watch it.

Always bear in mind the context of the page. If the video contains additional rather than essential information, then the play rate will likely be lower. If you are not happy with the results of this metric, try moving the video to a more prominent location, making the thumbnail more compelling, or altering the surrounding text. However, it might simply be the case that this particular video is unnecessary in its current form.

If your video contains a call to action with a link to purchase products, to subscribe, to fill in a form or to interact in some other way, you will want to monitor the click-through rate. In order to track viewers who, follow your video's call to action consistently through your analytics, you will need to add appropriate tracking parameters to each of your links.

If your click-through rate is low, it might be because viewers are leaving the video before reaching the call to action – if so, consider moving it to an earlier point in the video, or showing it more than once. Of course, if the majority of viewers are leaving quickly, you probably have a problem with the content itself, which should be addressed first. You should also make sure your call to action is consistent with the message and tone of the content.

Finally, there's conversion rate. This is the number of purchases, subscriptions, leads or other desired outcomes that can be attributed to your videos. This can be more complicated than it sounds. Few visitors will convert on their first interaction with you, so your videos are likely to be part of a process rather than the only content that potential customers consume. You will need to decide on your attribution model, and how video fits with it in terms of getting credit for the conversion.

Low conversion rates might be due to content that is not relevant to potential customers at this stage of the customer journey; missing, irrelevant or poorly placed calls to action; or the content not fully answering questions, which may impede purchasing decisions.

Remember, the metrics you should be focusing on are those that are most likely to help you achieve your specific goals for each video. Beyond KPIs that directly assess the performance of your videos, you may also want to look at the impact of video on other aspects of your wider performance. Does your video improve bounce rates? Does it reduce the number of customer support calls or complaints?

The answers to these types of questions can be researched fairly easily through testing. As with any digital marketing tactic, it is vital to look for ways to test and optimize for better results as you monitor your metrics.

When testing, remember to keep it simple. A/B testing that shows visitors versions of a page with and without video, or even different versions of a video, are relatively easy to set up and evaluate. The key is to change only one element at a time – if you do more than that, you will not know exactly what your visitors are responding to.

A/B testing can be especially helpful for assessing the quality of your advertising. An effective technique is to create different cuts of your ad, target them to different audience segments, and run A/B tests against specific KPIs such as engagement or click-through rates to see which version performs best.

Always focus on your business outcomes. As with KPIs, your optimization efforts should be focused on your long-term, wider business goals, rather than immediate - but potentially less valuable - results. For example, make sure you are not increasing click- through rates at the expense of lead quality by making your offer too attractive to the wrong audiences.

And importantly, benchmark against your own performance. It can be tempting to compare your view counts with those of your competitors, but this can be counter- productive. You do not know how well targeted or promoted your competitors' videos are, or how much they are contributing to the business. Instead, make valid comparisons. Set your own targets and benchmark your own progress for consistent, incremental improvements; and make sure you are comparing videos of a similar nature – it is not necessarily helpful to judge a video aimed at closing sales against one designed to spread awareness.

Finally, do not forget about other methods of obtaining detailed and meaningful audience feedback. In addition to using online analytics, consider using surveys or focus groups to gather authentic insights on your video content and the effectiveness of your advertising.

Do not ever stop testing! When you are clear about which version of a video is currently working the best, make it the control and see if you can improve further still by developing additional enhancements. Of course, this does not apply to videos with intentionally short lifespans, but you can still test the overall performance of platforms, placement, headings, calls to action, and more.

SUMMARY

H opefully, you now have a pretty good idea of the current landscape for online video marketing. But what about the future?

Well, there is no question that video marketing is only going to grow in volume and popularity moving forward. Viewership measurement technologies have developed to be able to analyze data with the help of artificial intelligence; and video can now be personalized through marketing automation. Virtual and augmented reality technologies are becoming more and more accessible, and the lines between advertising and entertainment are becoming increasingly blurred. In short, the video landscape is evolving, and we must adapt with it.

GLOSSARY

Ad Blocking refers to the use of software to prevent ads from being displayed on a webpage.

Ad Fraud refers to the manipulation of ad serving systems to inflate the quantity of impressions served. As a result, the buyer ends up paying for fake impressions, whilst the fraudster profits.

Ad Viewability refers to whether an ad could have been seen by the user it was served to. For example, if your ad is placed at the bottom of a page and the user does not scroll down far enough that it comes into view, it is not viewable.

Agile refers to an iterative way of working that aims to enable companies to react quickly to any changes in environment and customer needs.

Awareness: In the customer journey, awareness refers to the point at which your potential customer has identified a need, but does not yet know about your business, or that your products could help.

Brand Positioning refers to establishing or reinforcing the qualities that people regularly associate with a particular brand, in a way that helps define what the brand does and the benefits or purposes it serves.

Brand Safety refers to the issue of a brand's image being compromised by appearing alongside negative content.

Consideration: In the customer journey, consideration refers to the point at which a customer knows about you and your products, but is also considering other options.

Customer Persona: A persona is a fictitious profile that brings the characteristics of your target customers to life. These can then be used to help you plan your interactions with them; and to understand their typical needs, behaviors and preferred communication platforms and style.

Customer Journey is the stages and touchpoints a customer goes through in their relationship with a brand, from the moment they first identify a need they wish to fulfil all the way through to making a purchase and remaining a loyal customer.

Content Management System (CMS is software that simplifies the process of creating and distributing content, as well as tracking its performance.

Earned Media refers to the passing of content between consumers as a result of a direct experience with a brand. This encompasses all of the liking, sharing, reposting, and repurposing of content by customers.

Full-Service Agencies are companies which offer the full range of services for creating and producing video, from creative consulting through to editing and promotion; and often come with a broad spectrum of both equipment and expertise.

General Data Protection Regulation (GDPR) is a regulation brought into practice in May 2018 that standardizes the legal framework of data protection and digital privacy across all EU markets.

Immersive Video Also known as "360-degree video", refers to a video format in which content is recorded in every direction at the same time, creating an immersive experience in which the viewer can manipulate the angle of sight as they choose.

Influencers are people within online communities who command the largest followings within those groups. Sometimes they are celebrities, while other times they are just really good at finding and sharing content that their communities find interesting or useful.

Native Content: Sometimes referred to as 'advertorials' or sponsored content, native content refers to a type of paid media in which brands pay for their content - tailored to appear as a natural part of the surrounding content – to appear in a publication.

Programmatic refers to the automated buying and selling of media using software in which impressions can be bought in real-time based on an auction model.

Retention In the customer journey, retention refers to the point at which the customer has already made a purchase, and the brand is aiming to encourage customer loyalty and repeat purchases.

Sitemap is a file that contains a list of all of your site's pages and resources, and allows you to include information about videos. When made available to Google, this allows your content to be indexed.

Storyboard is a method of planning video content. A storyboard consists of a number of squares containing sketches or illustrations for each scene; accompanied by notes, brief descriptions, or references to the dialogue of the scene.

Videographers are professionals with good equipment and the expertise to film with appropriate sound, lighting, and so on. Clients may outsource to videographers to shoot their video content; however, the creativity will still be down to the client.

User-Generated Content (UGC) refers to any content made by users that can be uploaded to the web for the purposes of consumption, sharing, criticism or collaboration. It can be anything from a review or blog post to a short film or even a novel.

———————— ○ · ◉ · ○ ————————

ABOUT JULIAN DELPHIKI

Julian Delphiki is a pseudonym, created to safeguard the integrity of his personal identity and ensure that the focus remains on transformative ideas rather than the individual. This philosophical stance permeates every aspect of his work, from his senior role in a renowned multinational company to his more private collaborations such as one-on-one executive coaching sessions.

For more than two decades, Julian has successfully navigated demanding environments in both well-established corporations and cutting-edge startups in pioneering eCommerce sectors such as fashion. This extensive journey has shaped him into a multifaceted professional whose expertise is not merely theoretical but firmly rooted in practical application. As a seasoned professional, he has honed his skills across diverse functions—ranging from managing complex projects to leadership and activation—consistently delivering results that reflect his unwavering commitment to the success of every initiative.

His strategic vision and adaptability have made him a pragmatic visionary, capable of understanding the needs of the market, businesses, and audiences alike. Beyond his corporate career, Julian is the founder and principal consultant of his own firm, where he channels this experience to help organizations of all kinds optimize their operations and achieve sustainable growth. His work in this space often spans digital marketing, online business, and, more broadly, business management and productivity.

Yet Julian's influence extends far beyond the executive committee. He is also a prominent figure in the realms of personal development and philosophical exploration. As a lecturer in various universities and business schools, he is also a dedicated coach, devoting his energy and passion to fostering personal growth. His coaching philosophy embraces a holistic approach, carefully intertwining personal development with philosophical introspection. This dual perspective enables him to delve deeply into the nuances of critical issues in the social sciences. With a genuine passion for empowering individuals to reach their fullest potential, Julian engages in inspirational and transformative conversations while offering practical tools to catalyze positive change in people's lives.

The fusion of Julian Delphiki's professional and personal spheres creates a truly unique mosaic of skills, knowledge, and a profound commitment to enhancing individuals, organizations, and society as a whole. His ability to bridge the strategic demands of the professional world with the deep self-knowledge required for personal growth provides an extraordinary lens through which to understand human behavior and psychology, the direction of businesses, and the evolution of society.

This interdisciplinary foundation makes him a compelling voice, capable of publishing thought-provoking books on a wide range of topics—united by his core mission of fostering growth and understanding in a complex world.

OTHER BOOKS BY THE AUTHOR

La abolición del trabajo. BLACK, BOB and DELPHIKI, JULIAN. 2024.

Maestros del hábito. DELPHIKI, JULIAN. 2023.

Modern philosophers. DELPHIKI, JULIAN. 2022

A modern hero. DELPHIKI, JULIAN. 2022.

Folkhorror volume I. DELPHIKI, JULIAN. 2022.

Ad tech and programmatic. DELPHIKI, JULIAN. 2020.

eCommerce 360. English edition. DELPHIKI, JULIAN. 2020.

eCommerce 360. Spanish edition. DELPHIKI, JULIAN. 2020.

Content marketing and online video marketing. DELPHIKI, JULIAN. 2020.

Digital transformation. DELPHIKI, JULIAN. 2020.

Optimizing SEO and paid search fundamentals. DELPHIKI, JULIAN. 2020.

Social media business. DELPHIKI, JULIAN. 2020.

Tales of horror and history. DELPHIKI, JULIAN. 2020.

Web Analytics and Big Data. English edition. DELPHIKI, JULIAN. 2020.

Analítica web y móvil. Spanish edition. DELPHIKI, JULIAN. 2019.

www.ingramcontent.com/pod-product-compliance
Lightning Source LLC
LaVergne TN
LVHW051743050326
832903LV00029B/2684